THE LOUD MINORITY

PRINCETON STUDIES IN
Political Behavior

Tali Mendelberg, Series Editor

The Loud Minority

Why Protests Matter in American Democracy

Daniel Q. Gillion

PRINCETON UNIVERSITY PRESS
PRINCETON AND OXFORD

Requests for permission to reproduce material from this work should be sent to permissions@press.princeton.edu

Published by Princeton University Press
41 William Street, Princeton, New Jersey 08540
99 Banbury Road, Oxford OX2 6JX

press.princeton.edu

LCCN: 2019955873
First paperback printing, 2022
Paperback ISBN 9780691234182
Cloth ISBN 9780691181776
ISBN (e-book) 9780691201726

British Library Cataloging-in-Publication Data is available

Editorial: Bridget Flannery-McCoy and Alena Chekanov
Production Editorial: Debbie Tegarden
Jacket/Cover Design: Amanda Weiss
Production: Erin Suydam
Publicity: James Schneider
Copyeditor: Cindy Milstein
Jacket/Cover Credit: iStock
This book has been composed in Adobe Text Pro and Leviathan

CONTENTS

ACKNOWLEDGMENTS

From informal conversations on protests at political science and sociology conferences to the dinner table conversations of social movements with family members and close friends, this book is the product of many different voices that have been channeled through my raw passion to improve our understanding of American democracy. The journey I took in writing this book was long and arduous. Thus it was impossible to produce this book alone. There was a support group behind me that demanded my best, and who loved and encouraged me when my best was not enough.

I want to thank the Andrew Carnegie Foundation for providing me with the resources and time to write this book. As a Carnegie Fellow, I was introduced to a family of scholars who were passionate about addressing some of the world's most pressing issues. The fellowship also provided me with a large platform to draw greater attention to my research efforts. Alongside the institutional support I received, I had an amazing team of undergraduates and graduates at the University of Pennsylvania that provided an invaluable contribution. I am grateful for the efforts of Ava Barzegar, Candida Alfaro, Victoria Brown, Karina Miranda, Gabrielle Jackson, Sophia Elliot, Danielle Guy, Jillian Jones, Bridget Amoako, Skyler Rankin, Acacia Overstreet, Ashley Gilmore, Luke Yamulla, Drisana Hughes, Stephen Chukwurah, Sarah Simon, Michael John, Cary Holley, Makhari Dysart, Kaiyla Banks, Trevor Nunez, Jennifer Hu, and Amber Mackey. Their engaging conversations and lived experiences were fundamental to the completion of this book.

Several individuals have served as mentors from afar, not only influencing my thought process with their own writings, but providing sage advice when I needed it most. I am eternally thankful to Laura Smith, Stephanie Heilman, Christopher Parker, Michael Dawson, Jane June, Zoltan Hajnal, Martin Gilens, Jim Stimson, Robert Shapiro, Andrea Campbell, Paula McClain, Christopher Wlezian, Vesla Weaver, Sophia Wallace, Megan Francis, Chris Zepeda-Millán, Matthew Platt, Dianne Pinderhughes, Marion Orr, and Sarah Soule.

There are a few individuals, however, who served as my mentors and nurtured my development in academia. The sound advice and counsel I received from these individuals not only drastically improved the ideas expressed in this book; their guidance also shaped my worldview and allowed me to find my own path. I have a clearer view of the world because I sit on the shoulders of these giants: Fredrick Harris, Claudine Gay, Jennifer Hochschild, Vince Hutchings, Valeria Sinclair Chapman, Frank Baumgartner, Tali Mendelberg, Richard Niemi, Taeku Lee, Rogers Smith, and Amy Gutmann.

In the end, though, this book was only made possible by the advice, comments, criticism, support, and love that was offered by my coauthor of life, my wife, Leah.

THE LOUD MINORITY

Introduction

And we had an election for president that was determined on a slogan called the silent majority. Do you remember that? And if you weren't in the silent majority, you were in the loud minority. That was me [*laughs*]. And there was something wrong with the loud minority. It was like "us" and "them." And we've been having those "us" and "them" elections ever since.

—WILLIAM CLINTON, MARCH 4, 2000

"I would like to punch him in the face," Donald J. Trump bellowed into the microphone with a schoolyard bully stare in his eyes as a protester was escorted from a campaign rally in February 2016. The attendees cheered and applauded emphatically. Trump paused, looked out over the crowd, and took in the favorable response. As he basked in the appreciation of his followers, he smiled contentedly, pleased to have shown up the protester. It was clear Trump was not a fan of the protests. In that moment, however, Trump had done something more than just express his disdain for a disruptive protester: he established a political narrative. To the rambunctious crowd at the rally and some viewers at home, the protester became the villain of this American story, and the contrarian political message he espoused was the evil that Trump would guard against.

Trump strove to make it clear that this and other protesters did not reflect the public's concerns. Rather, they were isolated and erratic abnormalities—distractions that needed to be shunned. The rooting crowd of potential voters was "us," and the rude protesters were "them." This creation of a wedge between the public and protest activists, while far from original, warrants a closer look. In order to understand the contemporary narrative surrounding political protesters, we must understand the background story, which began nearly fifty years ago with the birth of the silent majority.

The Back Story

On November 3, 1969, President Richard Nixon appeared on televisions across the United States to make an important speech about the Vietnam War. The opening wide-screen video shot showed Nixon in the Oval Office, sitting at the Wilson desk. California gold-colored drapes framed the background, and the American flag hung behind his right shoulder. It was a classic presidential shot. He firmly grasped his prepared remarks with two hands. Repeatedly glancing downward at his written statement so as not to misspeak, Nixon discussed his approach to the Vietnam War moving forward. Despite cries for him to rapidly end the war, Nixon told the American people that he would not immediately remove troops from Vietnam but rather would offer a peace proposal. This peace proposal would include a complete withdrawal of all outside forces within one year, a cease-fire under international supervision, and the pursuit of free elections in Vietnam.

Toward the end of his speech, Nixon grappled with the opposition that he predicted would arise from those who disagreed with his plan. In an attempt to ward off criticism, Nixon recounted his interaction with a protester in San Francisco—an experience that stuck with him. The protester held a sign that read, "Lose in Vietnam, bring the boys home." Nixon acknowledged the freedom that the citizen had to voice this opinion. Yet he considered this protester and the activists accompanying him as belonging to a small minority in the nation.

Nixon used this experience as an opportunity to push back against antiwar protesters: "I would be untrue to my oath of office if I allowed the policy of this nation to be dictated by the minority who hold that point of view and who try to impose it on the nation by mounting demonstrations in the street. . . . If a vocal minority, however fervent its cause, prevails over reason and the will of the majority, this nation has no future as a free society." In concluding his speech, the president made a heartfelt appeal to those not participating in the antiwar demonstrations. He pleaded, "Tonight—to you, the great silent majority of my fellow Americans—I ask for your support."

Nixon's speech introduced the notion of a "silent majority" to many in the public. The term had not been widely used at the time, but it had a nice ring to it. It made individuals in the majority feel as though they had power, but they were modest and measured in how they implemented their power. If these individuals who sat quietly watching the political activism from a distance were referred to as the silent majority, then the protesters in the streets could appropriately be referred to as the "loud minority." Although the president did not verbalize this latter term, the implicit antithesis of the silent majority was a small group of whining complainers who did not reflect the true concerns of the American public or the reality of the times. Hence through his rhetoric, Nixon separated the concerns of protesters from those watching events unfold from the comfort of their homes.

The creation of this juxtaposition also established an atmosphere of "us versus them." But who belonged to "them"? Historian Rick Perelstein indicated that protesters against the Vietnam War constituted a wide array of individuals that included feminists, hippies, students, and even rock and roll bands. "It was everything that threatened that kind of 1950s' *Leave It to Beaver* vision of what America was like," said Perelstein (quoted in Sanders 2016). This wasn't just a distinction in political beliefs: the people in the "them" group were othered in more ways than one.

Opposition to Nixon's military actions emerged from all walks of life, but some of the most ardent critics of the Vietnam War came from the black community. Thus not only was the loud minority a statistical one in the eyes of Nixon but it also constituted a large percentage of racial and ethnic minorities. Adding the contentious state of race relations to political difference about the war only increased the distinction between Nixon's "us" and the protesters' "them." The negative connotation of racial division that became attached to the silent majority now reflected another prominent divide in the United States at that time.

By the late 1960s, the civil rights movement had won many battles, not least of which were the sweeping Civil Rights Act of 1964 and Voting Rights Act in 1965. The civil rights movement's attention quickly turned to the Vietnam War, however, when it became clear that a disproportionate number of African Americans and Latinos were returning home in body bags (Appy 1993; Baskir and Strauss 1978). Unfortunately, racial and ethnic minorities were more likely to be placed on the front lines of the war, and thus were exposed to a greater level of danger than their white counterparts. Furthermore, to civil rights leaders the deaths of many innocent Vietnamese children and destruction of land were unacceptable by-products of war. The fights for civil rights and international peace were inextricably linked.

Up until his death, Martin Luther King Jr. was adamant in his opposition to the Vietnam War. In his speech "Beyond Vietnam," delivered in the heart of New York City at Riverside Church, he encouraged fellow racial minorities to push back against the war. He went as far as imploring young college recruits seeking military service and ministers of draft age to become conscientious objectors, which meant they would refuse to serve in the armed forces due to a sincerely held moral or ethical belief that war is wrong. In referring to Vietnam, King (1967) stated that "these are the times for real choices and not false ones. We are at the moment when our lives must be placed on the line if our nation is to survive its own folly. Every man of humane convictions must decide on the protest that best suits his convictions, but we must all protest."

Indeed, protesting the Vietnam War became a priority for the civil rights movement—a fact well known to the American people at that time. So when Nixon asked for the silent majority to stand up and push back against the loud minority, the suggestion had a racial bent that insinuated a hard line of competition between voices in the minority community and broader US preferences.

The divisive "silent majority" term and racial connotation that it carried in the 1960s died out in political discussions over the next several decades following Nixon's presidency. Yet this hiatus from the use of this term in political discourse came to an abrupt close as the controversial millionaire mogul Trump entered the world of politics. During his campaign for president, much of Trump's rhetoric tugged at the nostalgia felt by some of his supporters for the "good old days" of America.

Walking along and fielding questions from reporters in 2015 early in his campaign, Trump turned to a camera to address the momentum he had gained in the polls. "You see what's happening and now they say I'm going even higher. The country is fed up with what's going on." Trump continued his explanation by resurrecting the famous phrase from Nixon: "You know, in the old days they used the term 'silent majority'; we have the silent majority back, folks." President Trump's revitalization of the phrase "silent majority" cleverly linked his campaign with that nostalgia. By indicating that the silent majority was back, Trump established that his supporters, "us," were the majority, and quite different from the disruptive protesters, branded as the less popular "them."

Trump would go on to make this tagline a staple of his presidential campaign, now rebranded and with more vigor. In a rally hosted in Alabama on August 21, 2015, he announced, "We are going to have a wild time in Alabama tonight! Finally, the silent majority is back." In Arizona on October 29, 2016, he declared, "The silent majority is back. In ten days, we are going to win the state of Arizona."

The Trump campaign and supporters even created signs that stated, "The Silent Majority Stands with Trump." These signs continued to be sold online on Amazon for the low price of $14.35 even after the election. What was once an implicit divide, alluded to by President Nixon, was now Trump's explicit line drawn in the sand separating protesters from nonprotesters. And if protesters crossed that line, they would be met with unwavering hostility.

Trump's words not only established a divisive political mood; they were demeaning and vitriolic to protesters. In June of the 2016 election year, Trump could be heard stating that he longed for the good old days when people could directly confront protesters and send them out of events on stretchers. Just a few months earlier, a protester was beaten to the ground and repeatedly stomped in the head by Trump supporters at a campaign rally. When asked about the situation, the then presidential hopeful confidently replied, "Maybe he should have been roughed up."

Even after Trump was elected to office he acknowledged that he knew there was a negative perception of the divisive term and how it related to protests. In remarks given at a roundtable discussion with county sheriffs and reporters, Trump (2017) stated,

> And a lot of people agree with us, believe me. There's a group of people out there—and I mean much more than half of our country—much, much more. You're not allowed to use the term "silent majority" anymore. You're not allowed, because they make that into a whole big deal. . . . But there's a group of people out there—massive, massive numbers, far bigger than what you see protesting.

Trump's words, like Nixon's statements a half century prior, indicate that protesters in the streets and the nonprotesters observing them at home have conflicting political perspectives on issues. It is therefore widely assumed that the act of protesting is the sole indicator of political discontent, and inaction is a validation of the status quo. The duality suggested by notions of the silent majority poses important questions: Do protesters remain on the opposing side of the political aisle from nonprotesters, or do protests resonate with the American public and shape political preferences? Do protests affect the outcome of elections and shape our democracy? This line of questioning rekindles an old debate regarding whether the silent majority, nonprotesters, is influenced by the loud minority, the activists in the streets.

This book attempts to answer these questions by making a bold shift away from separating protest and elections, and instead showing how protest activity spills over into the electoral process. Historically, political protest has been spurred by voices within marginalized groups, by those people who express the concerns of the repressed, and are seen as belonging to radical and isolated segments of society. Conversely, electoral outcomes in democracies demonstrate the will of the people and represent majoritarian preferences. As a consequence, political protest is often viewed as being a contrarian perspective to the outcome of political elections. I posit, though, that protests are a part of the social learning process, and act as an avenue of social communication between activists and nonactivists. In particular, protests serve as an informative cue that voters use to evaluate candidates as well as social conditions. The increasing engagement with social media by members of all social groups has allowed protest activists to interact more directly with citizens and politicians. Activists connect through popular media outlets, which disseminate persuasive information on the particular details of an issue. Protesters can now reach the silent majority in ways never before possible, figuratively moving the public ever so closer from the comfort of their homes to the activists in the streets. Protesters and nonprotesters now occupy the same rhetorical spaces for political deliberation.

Because protests place issues on the political agenda, and work to make those issues salient to the public and individuals in power, protests have the potential to shift voters' evaluation of political candidates. These informative protests can act as a mobilizing force that draws passion from constituents, heightens their interest in a relevant topic, and later increases the likelihood that they turn out on Election Day. At the heart of this influence is partisanship ties; voters use their partisan lenses to translate protest messages into ideological fodder that then propels their political actions. Not only are voters influenced by protest activity, but potential politicians looking to run for office assess their political chances of success by observing the level of activism in congressional districts. Conceived in this manner, protests are the *canaries in the coal mines* that warn of future political and electoral change. And it is the loud minority communicating to the silent majority that makes this possible.

A New Day for Political Protests and a New Audience: The US Electorate

Protests, social movements, and general forms of activism are operating in a different political climate than their predecessors.[1] Put simply, protests are more overtly political now than they used to be. More specifically, they are more connected to political parties. Protesters lobby outside political offices and interrupt Senate confirmation hearings. They descend on the Democratic and Republican National Conventions to garner media attention and shape the agendas of presidential hopefuls. Social movements have created political fights across a host of different issues for the public to see. The public is attuned to these political battles, and as these conflicts have become more political, protest increasingly relies on the public. The influence of protest on the public is essential if we are to believe Elmer Schattschneider's (1960, 2) eloquent message that "the spectators are an integral part of the situation, for, as likely as not, the audience determines the outcome of the fight."

In so many sociological studies of protests and social movements, the public lurks in the background as a reliable force and untapped ally that can advance activists' claims. The public can be particularly effective in helping to further a movement's political agenda. In a democratic system, the silent majority that stands on the sidelines is protesters' implicit link to government. These are the people who can make protesters' political goals reality—by voting. For all its importance, we know little about the public's *political* response to social movements.[2] I emphasize political response to highlight the power of the public to shape the political landscape and public policy. The public holds a precious place in political science for the influence it wields and is viewed as an unbiased arbitrator willing to consider all concerns. The public is an audience to which politicians can offer

---

1. Throughout the book, I use the terms "protest," "social movement," and "activism" interchangeably to refer to the same form of political behavior.
2. Kenneth Andrews, Kraig Beyerlein, and Tuneka Tucker Farnum (2016) make a similar point.

their appeals to circumvent institutional gridlock. For presidents, the act of "going public" allows them to speak directly to the public to create pressure on other branches of government to support the executive agenda. Protest activists also avoid traditional political tactics and address the public directly to ensure that their voices are heard (Lee 2002; McAdam and Snow 1997, 326). The public is a necessary component of social movements' political opportunities (Gamson and Meyer 1996).

Scholarly studies discuss the mass public as a broad entity, inclusive of all segments of society with all its different forms of activities and interests. This gives the impression that the public constitutes everyone in the United States—that there is an all-encompassing public that protesters are speaking to in their calls for social change. If we seek to understand the political consequences of social movements among the masses, however, then our efforts at focusing on the American public at large have been misdirected. The more politically consequential audience is a subset of the public; specifically, it is the voting electorate. While it is the voting public that we are concerned about, we oftentimes do not think about the distinction. Yet there are slight but important differences between the electorate and the mass public. The electorate is more politically engaged and politically active than the mass public. Most important, the electorate carries stronger partisan ties that make it more ideological. This allows the electorate to be more susceptible to the divisiveness of politics than the public as a whole.

What is more, the increasing political polarization within American politics has forced social change to be carried out by an electorate that has replaced a less pronounced mass public with markedly partisan voters. Consequently, to understand the influence of protests in American democracy, we must also turn our scholarly gaze to this new public that centers around the voter, exploring how the electorate is affected and impacted by political activism.

Surprisingly, the link between protest and our American democracy remains a gray area of uncertainty in scholarly research due to traditional disciplinary boundaries. Historians and sociologists have explored protest and social movements, but they have largely focused on movements' origins or what sustains them; they rarely draw political connections to electoral outcomes, leaving this terrain for political scientists. Political scientists have added much to our understanding of American democracy and US elections, but frequently these discussions eschew political protests because activism falls outside the bounds of formal electoral institutions and is thus deemed inconsequential—and perhaps better left to sociologists. This academic perception does not encourage sociologists to look at the political outcomes found in the electoral process nor for political scientists to study the sociology of American discontent.

Real-world events do not have the same disciplinary constraints found in academia, and we have witnessed the predicted shift that Bayard Rustin (1965) detailed in his appropriately dubbed book "From Protest to Politics." Several historical accounts embody this shift. In the 1930s and 1940s, political activism associated with the Townsend movement, named after Doctor Francis E. Townsend, who famously called for a universal pension for older Americans, led to the congressional election of candidates who supported FDR's proposed Social Security program (Amenta, Carruthers, and Zylan 1992). During the height of the civil rights movement, the 1964 congressional election ushered a new wave of liberal Democrats who were less conservative than their predecessors into the stronghold of the South, thereby establishing a "generational replacement" that some argue led to shifts in voting alignments (Black 1978; McAdam and Tarrow 2010; Bullock 1981; Fiorina 1974). For African Americans in particular, protests were relied on as a proven political strategy to confront discrimination and place racial inequality visibly on the public agenda (Lee 2002). Similarly, race has become a frequent motivator in recent years, as groups that resist progressive changes have mobilized and taken up methods of political activism to push back, reminding us of other periods of racial strife. Voices of political protest move beyond race to touch on many issues including immigration, gender equality, and sexuality. As protest begins to interact more heavily with politics, our democratic values are challenged and our American democracy inevitably evolves.

Throughout this evolution, the most fundamental trademark of a democracy remains the effort of elected officials to glean the "will of the people" and govern in accordance with that will. Political elections are often used to gauge this will, but protest actions can mobilize and guide the political sensibilities of the public. Protest can both represent and shift citizens' opinions. If we fail to consider how social movements are linked to the US electorate, we run the risk of misunderstanding the true political influence that protest has on American democracy. Thus we require a theory of political behavior that links protest activism to the electorate.

A Common Ideological Protest Voice That Binds Protesters and Voters

My theory of ideological protest expands our understanding of the political connection that activists have with the American electorate. The information contained in protest offers a basis for my understanding (Gillion 2013). Citizens rely on multiple sources to contextualize the happenings in their daily lives. Yes, we pick up the newspaper, reading the *New York Times* or *Washington Post*. While stories tell us about the latest dealings with corruption in Washington, DC, the increasing levels of poverty in our major metropolitan cities, and the most recent technological advance produced by Google or Apple, they usually do not get our blood boiling. They convey the news and are indeed informative, but their format lacks the passion and sincerity that would move average Americans to act. News broadcasts over television networks such as CNN, MSNBC, and Fox News are only marginally more inspiring. Even when political pundits on television networks offer impassioned remarks, it is still questionable how many other individuals resonate with the delivery of the message and this perspective.

Protest, on the other hand, is a form of news that is not only informative but evokes passion too. In conveying the passion of distraught and angry individuals who want to change the status quo, protest can bring up emotions in observers while suggesting that there is a considerable portion of the masses that also shares this point of view. Most important, protest provides an overarching and sustainable narrative about what is happening in society. This information frequently brings new perspectives to an old issue or highlights a grave concern that had previously been ignored. Protest narratives summarize the state of the world around us, and signal to the nation that the wrongdoings occurring on a daily basis may be so egregiously bad that they warrant an assembly of individuals giving their time and energy to push back.

The main question of this book wrestles with the ways individuals respond to and interpret protest narratives when they witness political activism. Citizens can have a spectrum of reactions to a protest narrative. For one, they can disavow the protesters as extremists who are out of touch with reality. They can also view the protest narrative as new information that updates their understanding of a specific issue and draws awareness to a potential concern. In addition, they can view the protest narrative as reinforcing their already-held beliefs and thus mobilize them to action. Much of what dictates the viewer's response to political activism will depend on the identity of the messenger, background of the person receiving the message, and characteristics of the message itself.

For individuals to participate in a protest movement, there needs to be a frame alignment whereby the citizens' interests, values, and beliefs overlap with the goals, ideology, and activities of social movement organizations (Snow et al. 1986). Some individuals do not participate in protest activity but still agree with the cause of the larger movement. This support from the sidelines requires a far lower threshold than what is necessary for one to get up and march in a protest, yet the frame alignment remains the same. If voters are to connect with protesters, they must find a common ground with them. This common ground is a similar ideological connection, built on partisan ties that citizens have with social movements. In this sense, protest is mapping onto partisanship to shape our electorate. Activism is not changing the deep-rooted partisan ties that are developed during childhood. Rather, it is temporarily fortifying those ties. Protest messages are conveyed to an American public that has become increasingly partisan, and movement activism provides a source of ideological fuel for this polarization, propelling partisan ties. This ideological connection to partisan allegiances leads to a mobilized electorate.

A mobilized electorate can ride the waves of protest movements and engage in politics that go beyond "in-the-streets" activism. People can donate financial resources to help political candidates that they believe will further the shared ideology of a movement. Protest-motivated voters can turn out to the polls to cast their ballot and change the power dynamics on the hill. Additionally, individuals can phone bank or canvas door-to-door for political campaigns to encourage their neighbors to turn out on Election Day. Highly motivated members of a mobilized electorate can even take matters into their own hands and run for office to challenge long-standing incumbents.

This conception of protests offers a revision of the idea of the mass public. The traditional perception is that those individuals who may sympathize with the movement but do not mobilize to participate in demonstrations in the streets are free riding. The term "free riding" is a harsh classification that implies these bystanders have the opportunity to reap the benefits that might come from favorable shifts in government or policy without having to engage in the work that protesting demands for hours or even days. Scholarship has implicitly labeled the silent majority as fitting this classification of a free rider.

I push back on this notion of the silent majority. Though some citizens choose not to engage directly with a protest movement by hitting the streets, they still may play an instrumental role in that movement's success. They do their part when they voice their preferences through voting. Even if the issues that protests revolve around do not reside on the ballot, politicians, especially once in power, can create political opportunity structures that are more or less supportive of protest messages (Eisinger 1973; Tilly 1978).

Members of the silent majority, particularly those belonging to the electorate, are far from free riding when they cast a vote. They become decision makers who can collectively create fertile political ground for movements to lobby their agenda to government. This argument presupposes that the voter and protest movement share a similar political ideological leaning. There are times, however, when voters identify with a different ideological position and oppose protesters' messages. In cases in which there are conflicting ideologies, voters are still active in the electorate, yet a differing ideological vote establishes voters as gatekeepers who are likely to elect a more confrontational government that also carries a differing ideological perspective than that of a protest movement.

The individuals in the silent majority may not speak with their protest actions, but they do bellow a boisterous outcry of social change with their vote.

Ideology Is in the Eyes of the Beholder: The Linkage of Social Movements through the Perception of Voters

Although there is a link between protest movements and individual Americans, as I have previously discussed, there are also links among social movements themselves. Scholars have long written about the similarities and common threads that connect movements to one another. One vein of academic thought sees these connections as marked by contention and conflict. Social movement organizations compete for participants' support, which often comes in the way of financial contributions and time (Zald and McCarthy 1980; McCarthy and Zald 2001). The organizations that propel and ignite the movement eventually find themselves competing with one another over the public's attention. This competition is viewed as a death blow to social movements as they move from the peak of the protest wave and head down what Sidney Tarrow (1994) refers to as a competitive spiral. Another vein of academic thought, though, sees social movements as building alliances that work together in a way that is mutually beneficial. Perhaps most crucial for drawing attention to their causes, movements work together to recruit participants. Activists from one organization move across movements to share strategies, information, and resources with other organizations (Minkoff 1997). When movements form alliances across multiple issues, they have a stronger base of engagement (Van Dyke 2003). These connections of similar interests, goals, and identities bring these groups together (Bandy and Smith 2005).

These discussions suggest that social movements have a choice on how they are linked together in the eyes of voters. Movement actors drive the contention or establish allies. Moreover, these discussions lead us to believe that protest activists are the ones who are creating the messages and frames that onlookers interpret. Yet the way protesters see themselves may be different from the way the public characterizes them and their protest message. Indeed, the way in which a protest movement defines itself along ideological lines is not the definitive classification of how the American electorate views it.

Conceptually, I argue that the electorate sees social movements as bound together and interrelated along ideological lines. Yes, hundreds of protests scattered across the country may have varying messages, different participants, and unique strategies. Nevertheless, they are inescapably judged and evaluated through the politicization of the American electorate. This is an electorate that has come to see partisan differences embedded within every facet of life and thus imprints this partisan lens on social movements' messages, thereby rendering the movements as an ideological collective. The movement might not want this classification, but it is bound to it all the same in the minds of a growing partisan voter. Indeed, all protests are ideological. It is here that this book offers a theoretical innovation.

Protests exist in a new partisan and polarized political climate. As such, what makes protest ideological is not the message or the activists of a movement, though it is true movements have become more closely linked to parties (Rojas and Heaney 2015). Rather, it is the interpretation of the voters who are embracing those protest messages that has increased the ideological bend of protest in the twenty-first century. The electorate, the masses of people who cast their ballots, looks much different than it did in the 1960s, when the silent majority was first called to the fore of the American political consciousness. The defining characteristic of the electorate today is polarization.

Scholars agree that polarization has grown and people now view many of their life choices through partisan eyes. Polarization in the United States is fueling partisanship, and partisanship is fueling how we look not only at social movements but everything in life. Even our daily choices have become partisan decisions—everything from whether to stay at a Trump hotel when you disagree with presidential politics to deciding to buy Nike shoes because they support the liberal agenda of Colin Kaepernick to eating a chicken sandwich from the Christian conservative food chain Chick-fil-A. We nourish these partisan ties through our selective daily interactions of only watching those cable news channels that buttress our point of view, or reading newspapers and sharing news links that reinforce the political positions we desire. Moreover, the personalized format of social media platforms, with their user-generated commentary, allows for the routine consumption of emotionally provocative content that ignites political anger in users more readily. We eschew those who have different opinions by unfollowing or unfriending individuals on these platforms, thereby even further narrowing our ideological exposure and reinforcing the "we" in the us versus them categorization of American culture. Partisan beliefs and ideological leanings have become so strong that they engulf other identities to form a broad political identity (Mason 2016). Protest messages live within this world and become politicized as a result.

The media plays a role in shaping the perceptions of protest as well, and there is a political bias in the media. For-profit media firms depend on audience ratings, and in an effort to keep their viewers and attract more like them, firms suppress or highlight news events that cater to their partisan viewership, which allows them to maximize profits (Bernhardt, Krasa, and Polborn 2008). These partisan frames disseminated by the media create depictions of protest events that fortify the partisan lens that voters already possess.

Individual protests movements rise and fall. Due to their ideological link to one another, however, the connection among different social movements allows for ideological longevity to be extended. One protest issue provides a liberal or conservative foundation, and another protest builds on that ideological foundation, creating a bond. Together these movements influence the electorate leading up to Election Day. Up until elections, protesters work to sustain their "interaction with opponents," as Tarrow (1998, 2) describes it. This book takes us on a journey through the various stages of the electoral process to show how the public's interactions with ideological protests matter for our democracy.

Contributions and Implications

There are several contributions and implications of this work. First, in considering the impact of protest on the electorate, we must recognize that the American public allegiance to a partisan worldview has intensified. This in turn has led to an evolution of how democratic concerns and grievances end up shaping the US political landscape. Today the American public is more politicized, and growing polarization has allowed politics to spill over into every aspect of our lives. As daily life has become politicized, we must come to terms with our newly created biases in order to understand how we relate to one another in the United States. That is what protest movements are about—engaging in deliberative democracy, where one citizen is speaking to another citizen, having a conversation in an attempt to influence and change one another's perceptions. What has yet to be explored in depth is the change in the ways this discussion now takes place. The electorate's response to societal events has evolved, and our everyday speech and interpretations have become partisan.

Through its theoretical and empirical approaches, this book grows our understanding of protest's impact on different aspects of the electoral process. By viewing protest as ideological, I consider the effect of protest to be more than a sum of its parts; rather, the awareness of the observer, the American electorate, changes the phenomenon itself to take on a particular significance. While scholars have previously sought to link social movements with electoral outcomes, this work expands our understanding of protests' political influence by including a long-standing political institution (voting) in the purview of movement influence. I chart a new pathway to understanding the impact of protest—namely, as working to bring about political change through electorate influence. In doing so, I adopt a view of protest that speaks across the disciplinary divide to engage not only with political scientists but also sociologists, psychologists, and historians.

Finally, this work argues that protest can signal electoral and political change in American government, thereby offering a refinement of how protest achieves success. Protest is not only able to influence policy decisions and politicians' actions directly but can also influence the political landscape as a whole by shaping who comes into office. As we will see later, protest can change the political actors by replacing candidates who may be less ideologically favorable to particular protest issues. In other words, protest alters its own political opportunity structure and is a foreshadowing of changes in government responsiveness.

Yet protest is not going to produce instant gratification. Protesters will not be able to immediately witness a congressional bill as a consequence of a protest event or watch the president sign an executive order on equal pay the morning after the Women's March. In this day and age where television commercials are avoided and conversations are reduced to tweets, our thinly veiled impatience and high expectations often demand monumental policy changes from protests for activism to be considered a success. While as Americans we want instant gratification, protest outcomes that take months or years to become visible are not failures, though some may see them as such. On the contrary, protest can play a role in longer-term successes throughout the election process. Protest plants the seed within the electorate today that will allow change to flourish in the future. Let's journey through the electoral process to see how this unfolds.

Structure of the Book

In the chapters to come, I aim to answer the central question driving this study: Do protests influence the silent majority of nonprotesters and subsequently shape electoral outcomes?

In chapter 1, I expand my argument that ideological protest plays an integral role within the electoral process and shapes electoral outcomes. I engage with previous theories that have minimized the role of protest in politics, but then introduce an alternative theoretical framework that highlights the value voters obtain from watching their fellow Americans express grievances to the government. The theory expounds on the overarching reach of protest actions in today's media landscape and how these political movements inform voters. The chapter offers a conception of protest that builds on previous works of informative protest activism, but with the addition of an ideological link to the electorate. More specifically, I assert that the ideological leaning of a protest is an important component for it to resonate with citizens. While protests on women's rights, for example, may address the specific grievances of gender inequality, these claims also fit within a larger appeal to equal rights and thus a larger grievance expressed by those with a liberal perspective. The specific topic of gun rights, likewise, might only speak to one portion of the conservative public, but an underlying value of self-reliance or security would also appeal to proponents of strong immigration regulation or those who oppose the expansion of the social safety net. Because voters seek out and establish information networks that correspond to their own political preferences, voters use protest events as an informative cue that reinforces their political beliefs. Protest actions signal a level of constituent discontent and vulnerability that is appealing to potential political candidates who might seek to challenge incumbents. This chapter discusses the realities of this theoretical framework for presidents and congressional leaders.

Chapter 2 charts the unprecedented rise of ideological protest and its geographic expansion over time. It begins with the adaption of protest messages by the dominant political parties, and weaves through the salience of protest issues since the 1960s and the civil rights movement, which served as the foundation of ideological protest. The chapter also expands its analytic lens to situate isolated protest events within the larger ebb and flow of ideological protest movements, juxtaposing liberal activism with the rise of allied progressive movements and conservative countermovements. I then discuss my definition of ideological protest and how to measure it. Afterward, using a novel data set that draws on multiple sources to capture protest activism from 1960 to 2018, the chapter shows the geographic distribution of ideological protests within various towns and neighborhoods across the United States. It highlights how the rise of ideological protests, observed by the American public, leads citizens to become more partisan over time. Most important, the chapter underscores that ideological protest can heighten individuals' personal ideology. I conclude the chapter by demonstrating how the political leanings of the national electoral map coincide with the fervor and political leanings of local protests.

In chapter 3, I explore the interconnected history of ideological protest and the national political convention. The chapter connects protest to the early stages of the electoral process, observing its influence well before Election Day. In doing so, this chapter speaks to the history of conventions—what they are, why they are important, and how their purpose has evolved over time. Stepping into the current era, I move beyond an observation of protests to gauge the perceptions and attitudes of actual protesters. Through this, I seek to better understand protesters themselves. What do they want and where are they coming from? The chapter reveals results from a four-month investigation that involved my research team walking alongside and surveying political protesters who attended the 2016 Republican and Democratic National Conventions. We find that protesters' intentions are not simply to directly influence the presidential candidates at the Republican and Democratic National Conventions but rather to use the political space and media coverage to draw attention to their causes as well as persuade the American public—specifically, the American voter. Realizing this opportunity for the media to spread their message, protesters come from across the country to have their voices heard. Citizens use political protests, however, in different ways depending on the political party they are targeting and their own ideological affiliation. Surprisingly, while liberal protests at a Republican political event are capitalizing on a publicity opportunity to persuade voters, liberal protests at Democratic events are an opportunity to persuade candidates and affect policies.

In chapters 4 through 6, I look at the actual impact of ideological protest on different aspects of the electoral process, as seen through voters' actions. In chapter 4, I begin by considering the financial benefits of protest in the early stages of the electoral process. I demonstrate that citizens respond to ideological protest not only through their vote but also with their purse. I use the Federal Election Commission's (FEC) reporting of donations to track individual contributions alongside ideological protests related to salient issues. This chapter shows that the financial beneficiaries of protests are those candidates who share a similar ideological leaning to the protesters. Consequently, liberal candidates raised significantly more campaign funds following liberal protest over a host of different issues than their conservative counterparts.

In chapter 5, I assess how ideological protest mobilizes citizens to turn out to vote on Election Day. I approach this by examining the actions of the Black Lives Matter movement in the lead-up to the 2016 elections—a contentious period marred by national publicity drawn to the disturbingly high number of unarmed African Americans dying at the hands of police officers. The chapter gauges the electorate's response to the Black Lives Matter movement, and finds that there were both supporters and critics. Yet the political implications are more intriguing than this simple dichotomy. Indeed, the liberal Black Lives Matter movement led to a conservative backlash whereby Republicans held a negative perception of activists. However, I show that these negative attitudes were not connected to their voting activity. Liberal voters, on the other hand, embraced this liberal movement, and these favorable attitudes were associated with increased voter turnout. More astonishing, Africans Americans—the most ardent group of Democrats—who lived in close proximity to protest activity saw a significant increase in voter turnout, but this was not the case for African Americans living in areas with no protest activity.

In chapter 6, I further explore my earlier theoretical argument by shifting the discussion of protests' influence from national activism to protests at the local level. I take this step to highlight that citizens are more attentive to protest behavior occurring within their own communities. Protests that happen in citizens' communities build on a larger understanding of people's own social environments. I show that protest can draw voters' attention to salient issues, educate voters on a topic, and lead them to vote for candidates whose platforms and ideological positions are consistent with the grievances expressed by protests. In particular, protests that espouse liberal views lead Democrats to receive a greater share of the two-party vote in House elections, whereas protests that champion conservative views stimulate support for local Republican candidates. Moreover, experienced or quality candidates are more likely to run for office and challenge incumbents when there is a higher level of ideological protest activity taking place. I provide a substantive understanding of protest influence on local elections by recounting the early political career of Abner Mikva and his electoral battles in Chicago politics.

I conclude the book by discussing what the findings of this work mean for contemporary politics. Given the influence that protest wields over voters and the electoral process, this work carries a powerful implication not only for an old debate in American politics on who has a say in this country but also for the contemporary question of what role citizen activism should—and does—play in governance. Protest is an expression of constituent discontent and thus an evaluation of a politician's performance. Nonprotesting voters also use protests as a barometer to assess the importance of issues in their communities and the nation at large, and may judge their candidates against the ideologies of protest. Thus protest becomes the pulse of American democracy, indicating the inevitable changing political tide that cannot be ignored.

1

Ideological Protests

THE PROTEST TIES THAT BIND US TOGETHER

We don't accomplish anything in this world alone . . . and whatever happens is the result of the whole tapestry of one's life and all the weavings of individual threads from one to another that creates something.

—SANDRA DAY O'CONNOR

It might not seem that we relate to one another amid the elevator music and earplugs we use to provide ourselves comfort in those daily moments of loneliness. But we do feel a profound need to connect with the world around us. Seeing our personal situation through the life experience of others gives us a sense of belonging and shared happiness. And seeing others' hardship also fills us with grief. This is the relation to others that protest fosters. Protesters lay out their concerns, reveal their lived experience, and place their hardship and strife on full display for the American public with the hope that they connect with the broader community. This showcase of human experiences is not ignored. Rather, protests appeal to our desire for connection and work to garner buy-in from the nation. The connection between protests and the public becomes the weaving together of life experiences that ultimately produces electoral outcomes. While not referring specifically to activism, Sandra Day O'Connor's words encapsulate this sentiment; the whole tapestry of protests reflects how our connection to one another can influence electoral behavior that shapes American democracy. When protesters gather to voice their concerns, these protests solicit a shared sense of purpose from others in society and encourage them to see the world in the way that the protesters do.

This chapter theorizes the significance of protest and its influence on American democracy through the electorate. It delves into the causal mechanisms by which activism is linked to voter activity. The theoretical framework fits within a larger discussion of political behavior and democratic deliberation. This theory, referred to as "the ties that bind," recasts our understanding of protests, transitioning from a focus on protests as belonging to one specific, isolated event or movement to considering a network of protest activities that address concerns across a host of issues. In doing so, this theory argues that multiple protests can become unified under a shared political ideology to both inform and mobilize the voter base, irrespective of the coordinating efforts of protest organizers. This theoretical framework describes how multiple protest responses to societal events energize the electorate, how this shift in the electorate's interest presents opportunities for incoming politicians looking to challenge the incumbent, and how this new political landscape shapes voting outcomes. Finally, I describe the social conditions needed for protesters' activism to strengthen voters' party loyalties, which in turn establishes the foundation for future electoral action.

Serious Doubts and Questions about the Role of Protest

There is an important conversation taking place about protest in America that includes the voices of scholars, political pundits, and even activists themselves. At the heart of this discussion is a valid question: Are the old-faithful actions of canvasing the streets and demanding change from anyone who will listen effective? Simply put, *do protests work*? This question surfaces periodically as protest increases in prevalence. Nevertheless, it is startling that this generation questions the effectiveness of protest, considering the extent to which it has lived through or been educated on the successes of previous protests that brought widespread societal change. Still, doubts persist in the most public of forums. Nathan Heller (2017), a writer for the *New Yorker*, titled an opinion piece, "Is There Any Point to Protesting?" Perhaps in an effort to sensationalize his point, or possibly a product of genuine pessimism, the opening line was even less hopeful: "We turn out in the streets and nothing seems to happen. Maybe we're doing it wrong." Suggestions have been offered on how to do it "right." David Leonhardt, writing for the *New York Times* on National Football League (NFL) protests, implored protesters to change their tactics from the controversial move of kneeling during the national anthem as a demonstration against racism to a more modest approach of wearing T-shirts. The suggestion here is that the mild version of tacit resistance that comes with wearing a T-shirt, which can also be mistaken for simply a fashion statement, is more agreeable to the sensitive palette of the American public.

Pessimism surrounding the impact of protest has surfaced even among political activists. This question of validity nags at individuals as they ponder whether their sanguine aspirations to bring about change have been squandered on a futile routine of walking for miles, carrying provocative banners, and holding up politically charged posters. Micah White (2017), a prominent organizer for the Occupy Wall Street movement, conceded the failure of protests in the title of a piece in the *Guardian*: "Occupy and Black Lives Matter Failed." His piece goes on to claim that "the people's sovereignty is dead and every protest is a hopeless struggle to revive the corpse. It is time to try a different method." White suggests that protest groups broaden their appeal to new demographics and become more inclusive because their issue-based activism has not brought the transformative social change that is desired from the movement.[1]

---

1. Moises Naim (2014), writing in the *Atlantic* just a few years ago, also offered doubts about the success of Occupy protests: "But most massive rallies fail to

Even among academic scholars, the foggy cloud of doubt has thickened. Mark Lilla, a public intellectual and historian, offered a stern criticism of protests when reflecting on the results of the 2016 election. He believed that the entire enterprise of protest as a means of effecting change was a lost art. Lilla (2017, 111) writes, "Protesting, acting up, and acting out will not do it. The age of movement politics is over, at least for now. We need no more marchers. We need more mayors. And governors and state legislators and members of Congress." Protests have come to be seen by critics as too reactionary and spontaneous, belonging to a form of folk politics that does not allow for the complex strategies and abstract thinking needed to achieve long-term goals and institutional change on a global scale (Srnicek and Williams 2015).

This suggestion seems overly harsh and contradictory in relation to the successes seen as a result of historical protests. Yet the contradiction between previous protests' achievements and contemporary pundits' pessimism is rooted in our evaluation of success. One issue that must be addressed and agreed on, in particular, is the definition of what "winning" looks like for protest activity and the accompanying social movements. Efforts to establish this definition might fail to garner a consensus, but we can agree on what it is *not*. Success through protesting is not one single thing: it is not *just* electing new officials; it is not *just* convincing elected officials to consider a new perspective on an issue; and it is not *just* enlisting a greater portion of the public to cast their vote in elections. Success can take a variety of forms. The multiple tentacles of political protest and their influence cannot be traced to a specific politician winning a campaign or piece of legislation being passed, though these events would certainly constitute wins. But there are other protest victories that emerge along with shifts in public opinion: mobilization efforts, agenda setting, the appearance of new candidates in the political arena, and the list goes on. Protest movements often have multiple goals and unintentional benefits (Andrews 1997).

---

create significant changes in politics or public policies. Occupy Wall Street is a great example."

The sway that protests have on political officials is undeniable; it is also visible on each branch of the federal government (Baumgartner and Mahoney 2005; Gillion 2012, 2013). Traditionally, presidents of the United States have been responsive to protest actions. Liberal protest activities increase the probability for activists to garner favorable discussions, press conferences, and State of the Union addresses from the president. Presidents also respond to protesters with direct action by issuing executive orders and memos directing cabinet members to address the issues voiced by protesters. Congressional leaders reflect on the issues that are occurring in their backyards, observing the content of protest actions, and adapting to the changing political and social climates in their districts. Accordingly, congressional members cast roll call votes in Congress that are in alignment with the prevailing sentiment in their districts, often coinciding with the message of protests taking place in their districts. Even Supreme Court justices are attuned to protest activity. Social movement organizations provide helpful information to the court by writing amicus briefs on important issues facing the United States. The salience of protest issues also increases the perceived importance of the topic and thus increases the chances that the Supreme Court will find space on its ever-increasing docket to hear a case related to a given issue (Gillion 2013).

Scholarship on the influence that protest can have on shaping political attitudes and the actions of voters is more limited than protest's impact on government, but several theories suggest a strong link. In both the social movement and public opinion literatures, grassroots movements are commonly viewed as viable means for shaping citizens' political attitudes. Protest activities can influence voters' perceptions through what Taeku Lee (2002, 69) refers to as "mobilizing public opinion," where citizens are informed by their peers. This bottom-up approach to receiving information can be more influential on citizens than the top-down delivery of the views that come from political elites. Informative cues from like-minded groups can shape citizens' understanding of issues (Page and Shapiro 1992). In relating political issues to the personal details of life, interest groups can provide the missing pieces of information that voters need to make fully informed decisions (McKelvey and Ordeshook 1986). The reason for this is citizens' engagement in interest groups, especially those that rely on protests, expresses some level of discontent that a portion of the nation has with the status quo. When this discontent offers insight into current policies or a politician's record, protest activities can inform individuals' voting decisions (Lohmann 1994, 518). Protest activists are well positioned to influence voters directly by discussing issues with neighbors at home or colleagues in the workplace, or indirectly by drawing citizens' attention to a salient issue (Claassen 2007, 126).

Evidence abounds on the political effectiveness of citizens demonstrating in the streets to voice their concerns. Whether or not a different approach, as White suggests, could bring larger or more clearly delineated victories is another matter. Still, this does not negate the fact that today, as they are, protests are indeed working. The underlying mechanism of *how* they work to mobilize the electorate and thus shape political outcomes remains a black box, and requires greater discussion and a clear theoretical framework.

Theory of Ideological Protests in America and the Ties That Bind

PROTEST NARRATIVES

My theoretical claims begin by shifting focus from a discussion of the influence of protest at the national level to protest at the local level, because citizens are likely more attentive to protest behavior occurring within their own communities. Local protests contribute to a larger understanding of people's own social environment, which can be informed by "casual observations," meaning simple observations conveyed by their surroundings—neighbors' dress, home, or behavior, for example (Cho and Rudolph 2008). These observations accumulate over time as well as repeated interactions and experiences in what Brady Baybeck and Scott McClurg (2005) refer to as the "slow drip of everyday life." The social context established in citizens' communities becomes the foundation of the social learning process that shapes their political preferences (McPhee 1963;

Sprague 1982). Though we often think of politics at the national level, many of the perspectives that citizens hold about politics stem from their local social environment, which later influences their voting behavior (Eulau and Rothenberg 1986; Huckfeldt and Sprague 1995; Kenny 1992). Some have come to recognize the social environment as a vehicle for increasing voter turnout by establishing norms of participation and providing social networks to mobilize potential voters (Rosenstone and Hansen 1993; Verba, Schlozman, and Brady 1995). Even simply being informed of the political engagement of people in one's community can increase one's own proclivity to vote (Großer and Schram 2006).

I argue that protest can become a part of the social learning process and act as an avenue for social communication. In particular, protest may serve as an informative cue that voters use to evaluate specific candidates in addition to social conditions. Because protest places issues on the political agenda and makes certain topics salient, protest has the potential to shift voters' evaluation of political candidates. Moreover, protest activities can educate the public on the particular details of an issue and unique ways it affects their community. Finally, protest can act as a mobilizing force that draws passion from constituents, heightening their interest in a relevant topic and increasing the likelihood that they turn out on Election Day. Steven Rosenstone and John Mark Hansen (1993, 218) contend that had "social movements been as active in mobilizing voters in the 1980s as they were in the 1960s, even leaving the social structure and the condition of individual voters unchanged, reported voter participation would have fallen only 2.6 percent, rather than 11.3 percent." Thus protests may not only be effective in shaping the opinions of habitual voters as they make electoral decisions but activism is also a resource for inspiring voters to remain engaged—or begin to engage, if they had not done so previously.

Political protest functions as another form of public opinion that informs citizens on important issues impacting their own communities as well as those around the world. It is difficult for citizens to be informed on every single issue occurring in the United States, and virtually impossible to give equal attention to each of them. Protests provide a filter for citizens, weeding out less significant issues and highlighting the most salient ones—and studies have shown that this takes place. When demonstrations occur in the United States, the issues voiced in those protests rise in importance on Gallup's list of what Americans consider to be the "Most Important Problem" facing the nation (Gillion 2013).

A crucial function of the informative nature of protest is its ability to spotlight issues that have been avoided by mainstream news outlets. Or perhaps, to correct the narrative presented by mainstream news outlets that have covered a particular event or issue so as to be consistent with the stance of aggrieved communities. In this case, protests can create and spread new narratives that challenge mainstream notions, serving as a free-flowing information conduit that updates the current narrative. Protest, in this sense, can impart collective narratives within the local and/or national spheres.

Political protest also helps shape a personal narrative for voters that will help them understand both domestic and national policies as well as world events in relation to themselves. When national tragedies and social strife strike, they are not embedded within a single political message nor are they uniformly interpreted. The shooting of multiple teenagers at a local high school could be interpreted as a need for increased funding for mental health care, but could just as easily suggest that the federal government needs to increase its efforts around gun control. Similarly, the rise of reported sexual assault cases in the workplace could signal an overdue need for companies and corporations to take complaints seriously and investigate all allegations, or a warning that society could soon engage in a witch hunt against honest men. It is the subjective interpretation of why these events occurred and implications that they hold that allows voters to understand and respond to such events. The protest activity that reacts to these moments provides an interpretative narrative of events and indication of the appropriate recourse.

A substantive example of protest narration comes from the 1960s, when public narrators, who came in the form of media commentators and political figures, attempted to depict the world as they knew it and not as it was experienced by aggrieved groups. During the height of the civil rights movement, Senator Strom Thurmond famously said, "The Negroes in this country own more refrigerators, and more automobiles, than they do in any other country. They are better fed, they are better clothed, they have better houses here than in any other country in the world." This statement came as a response to Martin Luther King Jr.'s speech during the March on Washington; it is the response of a person in power attempting to offer a competing narrative to the protest story being told by the movement that gripped the nation's attention. Evident in his comments is that Senator Thurmond did not recognize that being able to drive down the road or put food into an icebox did not offset the discrimination of being unjustly pulled over in that car or having your house burned down with the refrigerator still inside.

This political rhetoric and other sociopolitical events make an impression on citizens. And citizens' reactions can be gauged by public opinion polls, which also establish a narrative for voters. Although public opinion polls might capture the sentiments of a portion of the public, they cannot rally the raw emotional power of the populace in the way that protests do. Protests demand passion and movement; they are neither passive nor mundane acts of complicity. They are deliberate actions, whether strategized in advance or taken in spontaneous fashion by individuals who care deeply about an issue. There is no substitute for the rhetorical and visual power of crowds of people marching together, with signs and chants, calling on their representatives, all while engaging at times in contentious interactions with the police. These passions do not remain restricted to protesters themselves but rather can seep over into the hearts and minds of onlookers who potentially are sympathetic to the activists' cause. Protest narratives invoke passion for individuals that onlookers view as informative.

How protests are perceived is thus critical to their success. We often have a demanding perception, viewing the success of protest as requiring a lot of resources, whether it be time, funding, or personnel, to be effective. Chief among the necessary qualities we envision successful movements possess is strong organizational support. But protest movements are not always premeditated, well-conceived, organized groups of individuals with similar thoughts and preferences. At times, they are a spontaneous reactions to the situation of the moment. Nevertheless, when we view protests *exclusively* as spontaneous responses to a specific issue coming from a particular group, then these forms of activism are mere blips on the public's radar. We hear about a protest, find it to be an isolated event, and pay little mind to it. Yet when protests are strung together by a common unifying thread, they rise to be something more, assuming greater significance for the broader community, and embodying a movement that perhaps is more fluid and continuous than isolated incidents. The common thread that ties unified protests together is ideology. This conception of the ties that bind—an underlying shared ideology—allows for disparate protest events to have a sustainable impact on our democracy when viewed as a collective, without necessarily being supported by an organizational structure.

TIES THAT BIND IN IDEOLOGICAL PROTEST

We can view the question less as whether or not protest matters but rather, for whom does protest matter to the most? It would be naive to believe that protest actions send a signal of discontent that persuades everyone to adopt the position of the thousands of citizens marching in the street, the views espoused by banners with catchy messaging, or the passion invoked by activists. This simply is not the case. Protests are always about societal issues, and there are few, if any, societal issues that are agreed on unanimously by the American public. Thus protests along with the issues that propel them are bound to resonate more deeply with certain segments of the population than others.

Although not everyone will be swayed by protest actions or be compelled by the protesters' message, some are sure to be. In this world of myriad complicated issues, individuals gravitate toward the topics they find salient as they navigate through the world. Particular messages are more likely to be compelling for certain people. Hence for a given protest, depending on the issue and framing of the narrative, certain individuals are more likely to resonate with the protesters' message and more readily identify with the protesters themselves.

So how do marginalized protest groups persuade and enlist average Americans to join their cause? Put another way, why would an unassuming, white female who lives in an affluent, gated community in the suburbs care about protests that look to draw attention to the increasing number of deaths of black males in the inner city? We can pose the question in a different way by just replacing the main characters and protest event. Why should an older, heterosexual, black female care about protests against the government forcing a baker to bake a cake for a white, gay couple? Sharing a similar political ideology creates an unlikely bridge between us and those who are ostensibly different. Ideology ties us to individuals and situations that are removed from our own lived reality. These are the ties that bind individuals together.

A protest's ideological underpinning is what allows a protest that may begin with a narrow scope to have implications for broad political perspectives. For example, protesters who advocate for stricter gun control might in one demonstration communicate the belief that greater restrictions should be put in place to limit access to semiautomatic weapons. The public witnessing this protest in support of a specific gun control measure may see an alignment with a shared liberal view that the federal government must not stand idly by and watch the most vulnerable society members suffer such deaths; instead, government has an obligation to intervene. The same protest, however, can be interpreted by others as an affront to the conservative value of limiting government involvement in individuals' lives and allowing citizens to enjoy their constitutional right to carry—rights endowed by our nation's founding fathers. In this way, a protest advocating for gun control is transformed in the minds of some into a referendum on conservatism in general. By advocating for an issue in the public political space, activists (perhaps unknowingly) create alliances and oppositions along an ideological line that goes deeper than a preference for any single politician or policy.

The polarization of America has allowed even the most subtle and mundane concerns to be twisted into political fodder for the masses. Gone are the days when protest could remain independent from the partisan arena, and simply speak to injustice or wrongdoing. A new dawn has broken—one in which all activism, regardless of the specific issue being addressed, can be classified as ideological. The growing polarization amplifies the ideological signal, and helps individuals classify issues as either liberal or conservative—a binary distinction that was not so clean cut in the early 1900s. Today, regardless of whether one identifies as a member of either the Democratic or Republican Party, the growing political polarization in the United States makes it easier for citizens to distinguish a general partisan political line and align themselves with the side that more closely mirrors their own ideological orientation. Indeed, ideology is a means by which coalitions form across different demographic groups, serving as a link between those protesting in the street and those abstaining from protest.

This also means that people tend to feel connected to those individuals they perceive as similar to themselves, such as those who look like them or embody some of their own characteristics, especially in ways that deeply impact their own lived experience. For racial and ethnic minorities, this concept is referred to as linked fate. "Linked fate" is the belief that what happens to your racial group, or members in society who reflect characteristics of the group, has consequences that reverberate out to affect your own personal life circumstances. In other words, the fate of one individual is linked to your own. Scholars have shown that African Americans have the greatest sense of linked fate in the nation. The wrongful imprisonment of one black man will lead another African American to believe that they could endure the same unjust fate, or that their father, brother, or son might also be wrongfully imprisoned. A hint of this linked fate was expressed by President Barack Obama after the murder of Trayvon Martin, an unarmed black teenager shot to death by a vigilante neighbor. The former president simply stated, "If I had a son, he'd look like Trayvon," suggesting that a child of his could have likewise succumbed to this tragedy. As individuals, there is no more direct and personal way to assess a current event or political situation than through one's own lived experiences. I posit that a linkage between individuals is forged through protest as well, at a weaker though nonetheless significant level. Individuals see others voicing their concerns and challenging the status quo, and perceive a direct impact on their own life.

Within this interconnected conception, I view protest through a lens of bias and familiarity. As bystanders, we consider the issue that protesters raise, examine the people involved, and assess the geographic location in an attempt to determine our commonality with the protesters. The more boxes we can check off that match up with our own personal lives, the more likely we are to be persuaded by the protesters' message. The ideological linking of protest events comes into play again here. We can see these overlapping cleavages across protest movements that reinforce our personal political ideologies. And the greater the ideological overlap among the different groups, the more these groups have in common, and the more likely the message will be persuasive.

Ideology ties protests together across geographic space as well. There might be one protest taking place in New York City that conveys a particular message, while another protest occurs simultaneously in Seattle, Washington. Despite geographic distance, these protests do not happen in isolation from one another. As its vantage point, my conception of political protest takes a bird's-eye view of all the protest activity occurring in the United States. Americans who at least in some respect follow the news also adopt this broad perspective, not always by choice, but because the news cycle is inundated with events taking place throughout the nation. If we take a step back and move from examining a specific protest to exploring a collection of protests, then the broader message communicated to the nation changes and activism takes on a different meaning. How then do protests work in collaboration with one another, absent any direct contact among organizers?

Consider the Venn diagrams in figure 1.1. We can imagine Black Lives Matter, the women's movement, and March for Our Lives as separate circles that intersect. Each circle represents a different protest group voicing their concerns to the American public. What is the common thread of these different social movements?

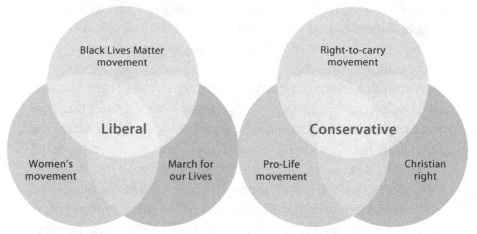

FIGURE 1.1. Sharing Ideology across Social Movements

At the center of this intersection, between all three, is liberal ideology. Additional similarities also exist across these various protest groups. For instance, the overlap that exists between racial and ethnic minority protest and the women's movement is that both women and people of color experience discrimination as well as unfair treatment in relation to their identity. These injustices allow them to reach a common ground and sympathize with one anothers' histories, helping, for example, individuals in the women's movement feel invested in the cause of Black Lives Matter. The same mechanism holds for those who identify with a movement's message but are not directly part of it. Beyond helping individuals relate and draw sympathies, the overlap is beneficial in invoking passion. At the core of protests' effect is relatability. I argue that similar aspects of experience and history (such as discrimination faced by women and African Americans) create fertile ground for protest messages to resonate across groups. The analysis of how two groups, and these two identities in particular, imbricate has been coined by scholars as "intersectionality."

This overlap of ideas and messages takes place on both sides of the political aisle. Protests calling for tougher enforcement of our nation's border and immigration policy and Second Amendment rights demonstrations share the common theme of rigorous adherence to as well as respect for the law. When the law is not upheld, these protesters feel some wrong is being done and that the country is changing for the worse. They possess nostalgia for the initial words of our forebearers and are resistant to a reinterpretation that results in change. Ultimately, a conservative ideology is at their intersection. This shared ideology can motivate one to vote with the same ideological perspective across several topics even if a voter is truly only passionate about one specific issue.

As highlighted by figure 1.1, I do not see protest as reducible to a single force within society. Rather, protests form a network of movements that work together when aligned under the same ideological umbrella. The question is not about Black Lives Matter and its impact but rather how Black Lives Matter is working in relation to the women's movement, immigration justice movement, and March for Our Lives to convey an ideological perspective and effect change. As these protest groups begin to form and their interests overlap, they start to create a broader political mood that increases the salience of the underlying ideology. In addition, as more protests arise within the particular political area, they link on to other ideological protests, further deepening the political mood. The lighter regions in the Venn diagrams indicate protest movements that have begun to emerge and share ideological leanings.

While the full structure of this illustration may not exist as such in citizens' minds, the average person does start to see these common themes emerge. This awareness does not need to be confirmed through citizens' discussions, though some political conversations echo this understanding. Citizens' perception of these multiple protest movements as being a coalition of protest activity happens organically. The slow drip of daily activism establishes the coalition of protest that leads to repeated interactions between voters and various activists who have similar ideological leanings. The liberal (conservative) signal is amplified as the network grows, which motivates liberal (conservative) voters to make it to the polls.

In this particular historical moment in politics and the unique political system of the United States, the unique identities and various ideologies that citizens harbor are condensed and applied to the two dominant political parties: Democrat and Republican. This allows protests to become more directly linked to government and institutions through their ideological relation to the party system.[2] As a result of the political polarization of the time, not all potential voters are equally supportive of a given protest event. In large part, this is because information cues resonate differently with different citizens (Bartels 1996, 204–5). When protest events are associated with a certain political party, voters who identify with the party are motivated to support those protest efforts and help the movement succeed. Individuals who self-identify as Democrats, for example, are generally supportive of the liberal views expressed in the civil rights movement (Button 2016; Luders 2010; McAdam 1982), the women's movement (Costain and Costain 1987; Young 1996), and the environmental movement.[3] Republicans, on the other hand, have embraced conservative movements, such as those of the Christian Right, antigay rights, gun rights, and pro-life activists. Political parties have attempted to capitalize on these differences by claiming issue ownership of these topics and including activists' perspectives in their party platforms (Fetner 2008).

It is quite astonishing that virtually every social issue has come under siege by politicians—politicized by a party platform and reduced to a partisan political leaning. Even for benevolent concerns that should be apolitical, such as providing kids with a good

2. Political protest often struggles to have relevance in a nondemocratic state. The reason for this is that authoritarian regimes can quell protest committees and silence voices, and political outcomes are frequently not a reflection of citizens' preferences but instead the idiosyncratic political ambitions of only the few who are in power.

3. It is important to note that southern Democrats were an exception to this rule early in the 1960s. As the black voter population increased in these districts, however, so did the support for civil rights issues among southern Democrats (Black 1978, 448–49). The civil rights movement also garnered support from black men who had previously served in the military. These individuals embodied a party paradox: a patriotic commitment to the commonwealth, on the one hand, alongside a need to challenge the racist status quo of that commonwealth, on the other hand. Christopher Parker (2009) nicely captures this duality through what he calls black republicanism.

education, there is a clear Republican approach and a defined Democratic one, and the two stand in opposition.[4]

As a way to strengthen ideological allegiances, political parties refine and reinforce the themes expressed in protests. Values related to discrimination, equality, constitutional rights, and preserving tradition are crystallized through the political platforms of the Democratic and Republican Parties. These messages are also echoed by political candidates and conveyed in campaign ads to strengthen party support (Mendelberg 2001).[5] This amplification of political messages serves to communicate to voters which party is most closely aligned with the prevailing political mood created by the contemporaneous collection of protest events. Because voters seek out and establish information networks that correspond to their own political preferences (Huckfeldt and Sprague 1987), voters may use protest events as an informative cue that reinforces their political beliefs and strengthens their support of a political party's ideology.

Liberal and conservative protests, in one form or another, are constantly present in the political arena. There is a tug-of-war between liberal and conservative perspectives as they vie for public attention as well as work to change the political mood of local communities and the nation as a whole. As the two forces are perpetually in competition, we can conceive of the countermovement to conservative protest as liberal activism and the countermovement to liberal protest as conservative activism. Both liberal and conservative protests also compete for political dominance on the public agenda. When both sides of the political aisle are equally vociferous in their protest behavior, the net effect is for the protests to be washed out, with demonstrations as a whole viewed as random noise. Yet as one side becomes more prominent, it begins to develop an inertia that attracts ideologically similar voters. This oftentimes operates at a

4. The stark differences in support for charter schools between Democrat and Republican politicians makes this point.

5. Politicians also have to decide whether to support a movement and consider the consequences of their actions (Amenta, Dunleavy, and Bernstein 1994). Politicians' efforts are driven by their constituents.

local level rather than a national one. For example, it could be that overall, protest conveying a liberal perspective is prevailing in the national arena, but if local protest activity is conservative, one may be less susceptible to the national liberal protest messaging because one is likely to care most about their own backyard. Protest is not only an ideological struggle; there is a geographic component that helps either ideological leaning to resonate more with particular communities. This raises an important duality for the geographic location of protest. Nationwide protests are essential for classifying whether a protest is perceived by voters as being liberal or conservative. However, when we turn to the effectiveness of protest mobilizing electoral activity, the beneficial components of geography shrink to local-level protest.

In a world where protest does not exist, voters are unmoved by political activism. Without narrations of protest, individuals lean on their own understanding and experience, which might not reflect the real world at large. To refine their understanding of the current political climate, they must instead rely on other means of information, which is delivered to the electorate in the form of public opinion polls, press conferences, campaign ads, and so on. This information can provide the gentle nudge that is needed to mobilize political action by voters. Alongside traditional means of political information, there are impassioned political cues from protest activity that narrate and interpret political events. Voters use this newfound protest information to develop a rationale for why they support a specific candidate or political party. Instead of a nudge, protest supplies a directional push to not only engage but also be supportive of a certain ideological side.

Thus as one ideological side (liberal or conservative) begins to dominate the political arena through heightened protest activity, the closest-related political party likewise dominates the messaging and increases the salience of their perspective of the issue at hand. For instance, as the network of liberal protest begins to intensify, it more loudly signals to and informs liberal voters' perceptions of injustice and fairness. These protests warn voters that this is an issue they should take note of and work to address, moving

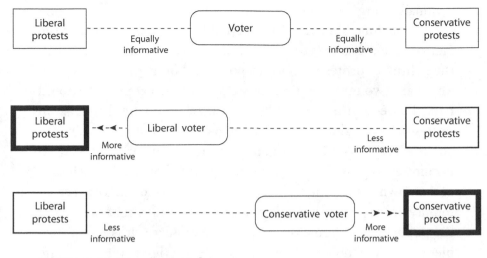

FIGURE 1.2. Direction of Protest Influence

voters closer to action. We can see this taking place in the liberal sphere in the second image in figure 1.2. Similarly, conservatives' call for limited government, and the preservation of traditional values pushes conservatives to act, as laid out in the third image in figure 1.2.

Within this conceptualization of protest, the overall vote share of politicians may remain unaffected by the large numbers of demonstrations. When both a liberal and conservative coalition of protests mobilizes citizens to the polls, they have a neutralizing effect on one another. Both sides increase voter turnout, but this renders the net impact of protest similar to the status quo of no action because the two sides counteract each other's effect.

There is also a timing component to my theoretical conception. Voters respond to protest activism most effectively within the time-bound period of the electoral cycle. They also interpret protest grievances in relation to the decision they have to make in the voting booth. Certainly, the influence of protests may move far beyond a specific election and shape broader attitudes on the state of the world. But voters, considering the options they have on the ballot, are often conditioned to evaluate politicians in the confines of the election cycle.

Finally, the geographic component of my theoretical conception bears repeating. Thomas "Tip" O'Neill Jr., a former speaker of the House, famously once said, "All politics is local." When reflecting on the politics of protests, there is a good deal of truth to this saying. There are two important reasons why ideological protest should have the deepest impact at the local level, and why the signal in protest is constrained at times by location. First, individuals care about what goes on in their neighborhoods, encouraging them to become deeply involved with and concerned about the social health of their own communities. When protest occurs in one's own community, it frequently spreads information about situations facing the population at home over a pressing concern; it is much simpler to imagine the impact of local political action in one's own life than the messages of national protest events that are taking place on the other side of the country. Second, voters' electoral voice is constrained to local-level politics. With the exception of national elections, voters are making decisions about their own cities, counties, and states. Voters are not only voting for governors and the president but also state representatives and school board leaders at the local level. These elections are directly linked to policies affecting specific geographic spaces that shape voters' lives and the lives of those close to them. Voters may ask themselves, *How can I cast my vote to change what is going on in the world specially around me*? Local protests are most effective at providing the self-interested answers that citizens seek because they inform voters of the various happenings in their backyards.

Capturing the Various Characteristics of Informative Protests

Following the innovations of previous work, I reaffirm here that protest is informative (Gillion 2013). Several characteristics of protests contribute to how effectively this information is spread to those who witness or otherwise hear about the event. In figure 1.3, I highlight the attributes of political protest that can be placed on an information continuum. In this diagram, the vertical axis depicts, in no particular

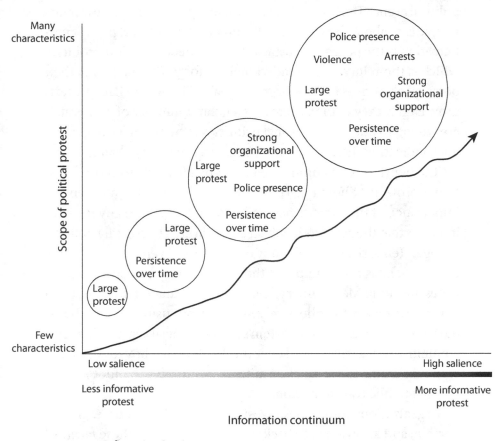

FIGURE 1.3. Information Continuum

order, the characteristics of protest that are communicated to voters.[6] As more traits of protest are revealed, this information shapes voters' overall perception of the protest behavior and increases the issue's level of salience along the horizontal axis, thus expanding the scope of political protest and its potential for influence.

The size and persistence of protest over time as well as protesters' organizational structure shape the saliency of the protest within the

6. Because each voter may assign greater value to certain characteristics of protest activity, there is likely to be a lack of consensus regarding which attributes are most relevant. Therefore each and every unique component of political protest is equally as important as the others. This line of thinking allows for a more general analysis.

political arena. These characteristics convey passion and how many people care about the issue at stake. Inherent in political protest participation is the potential obstacle of the collective action problem, which is the reluctance of individuals to forgo the pursuit of their personal objectives in favor of group goals (Chong 1991). As protests grow larger, they demonstrate that a greater number of individuals are willing to put aside personal priorities to pursue a more general goal, indicating their true commitment to the issue at hand.

The depth of this commitment can be gleaned from the duration of protests.[7] Short-lived political action reflects the momentary importance of the topic, whereas a constant appeal to government indicates that the activists involved are dedicated to creating political change. Hence the size and duration of protest events offer valuable information, as the example of the Montgomery bus boycott illustrates. Blacks in Montgomery, Alabama, coordinated their efforts in massive numbers to collectively abstain from using the city buses during a protest against the system's policy of racial segregation. This commitment was reinforced over the 381 days that boycotters spent enduring cramped car rides or miles of commuting by foot instead of using public transportation.

Organizations sometimes invest their financial resources, membership, and knowledge to back political action, and these facets of a protest's organizational structure enhance the involved activists' credibility with politicians. For instance, when a teachers' union, Greenpeace, Planned Parenthood, or the National Association for the Advancement of Colored People (NAACP) are connected to a protest, their endorsement provides greater legitimacy to the claims expressed in these events.

There are more contentious aspects of protest that are also salient components of information. The potential of protests to include violence such as a property being damaged at an event,

---

7. Both the size of protest and commitment that protesters have to issues are also components found in Charles Tilly's (1996, 53–54) WUNC acronym, which abbreviates "worthiness, unity, numbers, and commitment." The numbers and commitment seen in protest are displays that provide information to and attract attention from local observers.

police arrests, and even personal injury convey the ardor that protesters have for an issue. Whether instances of force are instigated
by participants or withstood by activists, onlookers come to real-
ize the magnitude of the concern that compelled protesters to hit
the streets in the face of possible force. These characteristics show
protesters' investment in the issue that spurred them to take action
beyond participating in elections, leading them to give their time
and at moments risk personal sacrifice in pursuit of a collective
aim. These characteristics of political protest work in tandem with
one another to inform voters. And these various forms of information can build up to mobilize political participation from voters in
the silent majority.

Electoral Backlash

The influence of protests is not limited to those who share an ideological stance with the protest message. Protests also engage individuals with opposing views, mobilizing and motivating those who
disagree with protesters to push back against them and the stances
they take. There is no denying the existence of backlash, even in
the mild sense of individuals disapproving of protest activism as a
viable means to elicit change. Yet I maintain that the backlash from
the silent majority is not motivating enough to mobilize these voters electoral actions, so it does not offset the positive influence of
protest. It is important to note that I am narrowing my focus to the
electoral backlash and not counterprotest movements, which can
often occur in response to ideological protest. The electoral response
of the silent majority, however, is different. The reason for this is
because the backlash to protest stems from multiple sources, including some that are unrelated to the policy issue that protesters hope
to accomplish. In some cases, the protest backlash is motivated by
the disdain bystanders have for the protesters themselves. Critical
views about the facts of the protest (thoughts like "I just don't think
that group should be out there doing that") may generate pushback
against the group that is protesting. Negative sentiment such as disdain or hatred might be there, but policies channeling this disdain

to specific groups are unlikely to be on the ballot and thus unlikely to motivate voters to the polls in the same way that issue-driven activism will.

It is not only that some individuals experience discontent about the protesters themselves. This discontent can extend to the very action or method of protest itself. Take, for example, the backlash against the protest carried out by NFL players during the national anthem in the 2017 and 2018 seasons. In order to draw attention to the violence committed against African American men by police officers, players began kneeling during the anthem. Like other popular protest movements, these players garnered sympathy for their cause, but not everyone agreed. Some argued against the very existence of protest in that venue, saying politics has no business in football. There was also a perception that the form of protest, kneeling during the national anthem, was disrespectful to the nation and suggestive of a lack of honor for this country. This does not necessarily mean that those with this perception disagree that African Americans are disproportionately targeted by police, or that police brutality and discrimination remain a problem. They might actually agree with these views. But still, they disagree with the protesters' method: How *dare* you protest the national anthem? This negative sentiment overpowers any sympathetic feelings they might have regarding the issue highlighted by the protest and becomes a separate concern in itself. The backlash becomes about how people ought to behave in public spaces. It is unlikely to stick with voters throughout the election cycle and mobilize individuals to vote against the issue raised by the protest.

In the electorate, there exist segments of backlash and support that are consequential for political outcomes. Protest matters in American democracy because it provides an avenue for activists to exercise their voices politically, outside the normal electoral process that takes place at most once a year. When these protest movements are tied to other political actions, they have the potential to resonate more deeply than if they had occurred in isolation. In this way, protests link to other protests to keep important issues on the radar of the American electorate and work together to motivate voters to act on the passion that the protests inspired.

Expectations

The ideological leanings of political activism can heighten social and political issues for those who have similar ideological leanings. This is the essence of the theoretical framework of "the ties that bind." This theory leads to several predictions regarding the outcomes of ideological protest. The major expectations are as follows:

- *As the number of liberal (conservative) protests increases in a community, liberal (conservative) politicians are more likely to secure greater resources in terms of raising money and receiving support from their political party.*
- *As liberal (conservative) protests increase in a community, liberal (conservative) voters are more likely to turn out on Election Day.*
- *Increases in protest activity that expresses a liberal (conservative) position is associated with a greater share of the two-party vote for the Democratic (Republican) candidate.*

Chapters 4 through 6 empirically test the validity of these claims.[8]

Conclusion: Looking Ahead to a Protest in a More Connected World

When citizens go to the polls, they reflect on the world around them and draw on the signals that indicate the health of the nation. These cues can come from many places and take different forms. James Carville famously said, "It's the economy, stupid," and many certainly look to economic factors to aid them in deciding how to cast their vote. Others may consider the president's approval rating as a barometer for not only how citizens evaluate the commander in chief but also to what extent the president's political party is supported. Others might believe that voters already have their minds made up

---

8. As is the standard methodological approach taken by social scientists, I use statistical models to explore these claims. While statistical models cannot validate causality, they can demonstrate a strong relationship between the variables of interest.

and that these views are entrenched to such a degree that there is nothing that can be done to change them.

In the midst of all these considerations lies a desire to know about the welfare of one's neighbor. There is no substitution for engaging in conversations with one another, but we live in a society that has allowed elevator music to drain out the awkwardness of our isolation in confined spaces with one another. Protest changes this dynamic by inspiring the public to engage in conversations, if not actions, about salient social and political issues. The loud minority discusses the nation's concerns with the electorate and solicits its support. Protesters are not only connected to voters through their underlying ideology but are linked through their language and how they frame messages too. Although this messaging tends to resonate with some groups more than others, the overall ideology of protest can be mobilizing for voters.

Of all the ways that activists can communicate their goals and criticisms to society, protest activity has the potential to be uniquely effective. Demonstrators voice their concerns on a grand stage, allowing voters to understand the impact of policies on their lives and the potential consequences of their changes. Protest is rallying like-minded voters, antagonizing the opposition, or informing those who are undecided—and often it accomplishes all three of these things at once. The influence that protest has on the electoral process reaches far beyond the decision that citizens make in voting for a particular candidate in the elections. Protest also impacts voter turnout, campaign contributions, and even who decides to run for office. In the chapters to come, this book will consider the entire electoral process—not just whether the electorate votes.

More important, this work demonstrates how protest's increased frequency has changed the way that the public views and engages with political activism. Protests are no longer perceived as a practice reserved for "random, crazy" individuals or those on the fringes. Today we see families engaging in protest, coworkers carpooling to rallies after a workday, and teenage friends joining movements together through social networks. We see easily relatable individuals in mainstream society, or those with whom we see ourselves sharing a common bond and similar experiences. It is these ties that make protest different and more effective—now than ever before.

2

The Making of
Ideological Protests

I think more of the machine within the GOP is gonna
understand this "we the people" message is rising, and is
resonating throughout with independents, with hard-core
conservatives, with moderates, because it's just so full of
common sense and time-tested truths that can put the
economy on the right track. That heaven forbid that the GOP
machine strays from this message—if so, [the] GOP is through.

**—SARAH PALIN, AFTER SPEAKING AT A TEA PARTY RALLY IN
RENO, NEVADA, OCTOBER 10, 2010**

During the 2010 midterm election cycle, political protest had, seem-
ingly overnight, unequivocally changed the direction of the Republican Party. Protesters' voices became the party's voice, and that voice
was unapologetically ideological. This was on full display during the
closing weeks of the midterms when candidates and political opera-
tives made their final pitches to constituents on the campaign trail.
A familiar voice led the charge to unite protest with the party: the
2008 vice presidential candidate and former governor of Alaska,
Sarah Palin. Palin had become a prominent spokesperson for the Tea

Party movement. She seized on the protest movement's message of fiscal conservatism, smaller government, and a reluctance to allow the federal government to intrude on state affairs. She carried these ideals to conservative voters throughout the country—on a tour bus no less. This protest message, drenched in a right-wing ideological bent, resonated with the electorate.

It was not long before the Tea Party movement and its protests became entrenched within the Republican Party establishment. John Boehner, the Republican Speaker of the House who had recently taken the gavel from Democrat Nancy Pelosi in 2010 as a result of the elections, reached out to members of the Tea Party to express his unwavering support for their movement. In a Skype call, Boehner told the activists, "I'll never let you down." Evident through this call was Boehner's awareness that the GOP's electoral future was connected to the Tea Party. His words were the culmination of fierce conservative protests that had led to the first party change in the lower chamber of Congress since 2006, with Republicans regaining control of the House of Representatives. The shift in power was so dramatic that President Obama famously remarked that his Democratic Party had simply received a "shellacking," harking back to when his Republican predecessor George W. Bush described the 2006 wipeout of House Republicans as a "thumping." The Tea Party protests invoked a conservative message that awoke Republican voters and was successful enough to demand that Republican elites get on board or risk their electoral fortunes. In the case of the Tea Party movement, protest actions had become inseparable from a conservative ideology and the Republican Party itself.

In the specific moment of 2010, the most prevalent protest events happened to be conservative, and those onlookers embracing the message happened to come from the Republican Party and its base. Yet the wedding of protests' ideological messages and the political party system was far from unusual in the broader context of political protest. Actually, the regularity of historical occurrences of political parties absorbing and representing protest movements has made the link between political parties and protests the new norm. In this chapter, I trace the origins of the ideological bent of protest movements. We will see that ideological protest is a relatively new phenomenon that emerged in the 1960s and has strengthened over time. Shifting political norms and political perceptions in society brought protest in closer alignment with specific political parties. As the nation became more politically polarized, citizens began to interpret diverse topics as wedge issues that belonged to either the Democrat or Republican Party camps. Political parties, seeking to maximize their electoral influence, selectively co-opted those protest issues in an effort to grow and enthuse their respective bases.

The various issues that gained national prominence through protests came in historical waves, rising to importance for a short period of time and then fading from America's attention. At their peaks, however, these protest waves heightened an ideological view that led average citizens to deepen their partisan engagement as well as embrace a specific party and its ideology. This chapter shows us that the link between protest and voter behavior is seen even beyond Election Day results, though it is most pronounced in that moment. Citizens embrace the constant flow of information coming from political activism over the course of the entire election year, and as they evaluate protest messages through the lens of their chosen political party, they strengthen that party association. This bond between protest and party ideology continuously helps to build momentum until voters have an opportunity to act on their motivations at the voting booth. The links between protest messages mapping onto partisanship are deep and ongoing. The growth of ideological protests in American society is what has allowed citizens' activism to shape the attitudes of the electorate.

Ultimately in this chapter, I introduce the concept of ideological protest in action, providing a broad notion of what ideological protest means and what it can produce. I introduce a way to measure ideological protest and chart how it has changed over time. Combined with a clearer understanding of how ideological protest is shaping our perceptions and attitudes, here we build familiarity with the topic historically and empirically, allowing us to better consider its implications.

Sorting Protest Messages into the Democrat and Republican Parties

When you see a protest or social movement, national political parties are not far behind to champion the issues being expressed. It was actually on the backs of a social movement that partisanship was defined or, more accurately, redefined. Both major political parties clamored to claim ownership of efforts to address racial inequality in the 1960s. During the 1960 presidential election, John F. Kennedy and Nixon each took their respective parties' lead in advocating for equality through messages laid out in both parties' platforms. But it was Kennedy's symbolic ties to the movement that gave his party the advantage. His public call to Coretta Scott King in 1960 inquiring about the recent arrest of her husband, Martin, cemented the Democratic Party as being more closely related to the issue of racial equality (Carmines and Stimson 1989, 39). The Democratic efforts of Lyndon B. Johnson to pass the 1964 Civil Rights Act hardened the party's relationship to issues of race. Many prosegregation southern Democrats, referred to as "Dixiecrats," exited the Democratic Party as a consequence. President Johnson famously stated that in supporting the Civil Rights Act, the Democrats had "lost the South for a generation." The issues related to racial equality highlighted in the civil rights movement continued to shape partisanship. This was especially true in the South, the geographic area where protest was most intense, and where the sentiments of racial antagonism that were ignited by activism on racial inclusion were also linked more closely with the Republican Party (Valentino and Sears 2005). The issues voiced in protest became the source of partisanship realignment as protesters and counterprotesters broke along party lines.

On the heels of a major party alignment, the United States witnessed the consequences of one of the most intense protest movements in American history. These protest actions would profoundly shake the foundations of the party system and political allegiances, forcing individuals to sever political party ties and refocus their ideological goals for political actions. Just as citizens' association with a political party (which brought on a new social identity) began to take hold in the 1960s (Johnston 2006), protest actions began to intensify. The connection between ideology and partisanship also intensified. Moving into the 1970s, ideology became congruent with partisanship, with liberals overwhelmingly identifying with the Democratic Party and conservatives seeing themselves as Republicans (Levendusky 2009; Abramowitz 2010).

The political ideology of liberals and conservatives is not the only identity that has been sorted along party lines. Individuals carry their own social identities informed by gender, race, or religion, among other personal characteristics. Over time, however, people's social identities have merged with their partisan identities. In other words, an individual's multiplicity of social identities has become encompassed within a singular partisan identity. This single political and social identity rarely can be represented by both parties, and thus it is difficult for partisans to find common ground (Mason and Wronski 2018).[1] As combinations of social identities move into alignment with one another, they are capable of motivating political action and creating stronger political ties (Mason 2015, 2016). When individuals with similar identities come together for political change, they form a collective identity, and individuals within the collective find support and encouragement of those identities (Klandermans 2014). Protest messages are not personal identities, but like individual identities, they can converge into something more encompassing.

Protest messages are often entangled with social identities because activists have their own unique identities and those become politicized (Klandermans 2014, 4). The inseparable link between the protest movement's collective identity and the protest message makes it susceptible to the politicizing of identities. Social identities become politicized when the collective social group identities demand change from the government (Huddy 2015). As such, the *message* voiced by collective identity groups also becomes politicized

---

1. And though Democrats have been described as being more closely associated with identity politics, it is the Republican Party that is more closely related to the social identities of whiteness and Christianity (Mason and Wronski 2018).

when it is a message directed to the government. This makes it easier for the public to sort political messages into political parties.

Protest activity also draws attention to concerns that allow voters to better understand an issue through the ideological frame of activists. Voters later rely on this newfound knowledge to make informed decisions about political candidates. The time it takes for voters to obtain and process information that moves them closer to a specific political ideology as a consequence of protest is not spontaneous. The electorate begins to embrace the political ideology that it sees in political activism over time and as it is repeatedly exposed to political messaging. A slow drip of information and knowledge impresses on the attitudes of voters. In many instances, voters do not have a primary outlet to express this shifting sentiment, and that is why we see the strong relationship between protest activity and political engagement during elections. Yet outside Election Day, and actually leading up to elections, individuals harbor these same ideological sentiments, though largely unbeknownst to others. These ideological sentiments continue to grow as more protests are conducted across the nation. Citizens internalize the messages of ideological protests and channel them through their own party allegiances throughout the year.

Put simply, protest moves individuals to cultivate the seed of their existing partisanship. Liberal protests move those who are ideologically predisposed to embrace the activists' message in a liberal direction, leading them to more strongly identify with the Democratic Party. The reverse is true for conservative protests and the Republican Party.

Activism Messages and Issue Ownership: Which Party Owns Which Protest Issues?

Up to this point I have spoken about ideological protests as fitting in two bins, where protest issues can convey a liberal or conservative perspective. But a big question is left unanswered: How do protest issues establish these ideological leanings? Protests do not always start off being ideological. Protest messages are often co-opted by news outlets, political pundits, and politicians who seek to make sense of protesters' concerns in light of the current political environment. The strange bedfellows of activists challenging the government's status quo, political parties, in particular, embrace protest messages and imprint their ideological leanings on activism.

Activists themselves rarely declare party alignment. Instead, the ideological leanings of protest issues are formed through the public's conception of issue ownership. Issue ownership is a theory that originated with the political scientist John Petrocik. Petrocik's (1996) theory states that politicians are more successful at attracting voters when they can present voters' primary concerns in terms of a problem that the party is best suited to handle. Hence we can conceive of issue ownership as how one party becomes the party of gay rights, or the party of race. Scholars simplify this notion by stating that "Democrats 'own' some issues; Republicans 'own' others" (Petrocik, Benoit, and Hansen 2003–4).

Petrocik's theory does not classify protest per se but rather the issues themselves. Historically, public opinion polls have viewed Democrats as being better equipped to address discrimination and intergroup problems. These problems and the party's perceived skill at addressing them give Democrats an electoral advantage when those issues are on the top of voters' minds. Republicans are viewed as being good for the economy because they are strong on financial issues involving taxes and spending. When Republican politicians run on these issues, historically they are more likely to be successful.

Both conservative and liberal social protest movements have advocated for policy changes tied to issues that are similarly espoused by the political parties. For conservatives, the arrival of the New Right in the 1970s marked a turning point for social movements, which in the 1960s had been inconsequential in terms of their influence (Blee and Creasap 2010). This New Right, bearing a broad goal of returning "America to political, economic, and moral strength," was notably grassroots in nature, bringing together fragmented conservative interests, including "free market enthusiasts, libertarians, anticommunists, and social conservatives," and mobilized individuals from a range of socioeconomic backgrounds including the middle class (Blee and Creasap 2010, 272; Durham 2000; Johnson 2000; McGirr 2015).

Kathleen Blee and Kimberly Creasap (2010) suggest that there were two primary contextual factors that shaped the dramatic success of the New Right. The first was the unification of social and economic conservatives, facilitated by a change in social conservatives' language away from racially explicit rhetoric following the civil rights activism of the 1960s. This paved the way for their alliance with free market conservatives who were less prone to the use of outwardly white supremacist speech. The second factor was increased political engagement by religious conservatives, particularly evangelical Protestants. Catholics were also involved, though their activity was mainly limited to movements resisting lesbian, gay, bisexual, and transgender (LGBT) equality and abortion. The influence and involvement of evangelical Christians grew in the 1980s as this New Christian Right fought back against secularization and advocated for a "repoliticization of religion" (Blee and Creasap 2010, 273; Jacobs 2006; Burack 2008; Fetner 2008).

Republicans' political identity has become nearly synonymous with their religious values. Religion has served, and continues to do so, as a bond as well as source of power and unification for conservative movement builders and many Republican politicians. While the Tea Party's subsequent rise to power was not framed through an explicitly religious lens, nor is it formally a religious organization, it is difficult to deny that religion underscores its policy positions (Clement and Green 2011). The ties among protest activists and members of the Republican Party have strengthened as conservative movements proliferated.

On the liberal side, the tying bond within the Democratic camp has been the call for justice in response to discrimination against marginalized groups. As King (1994) stated in his well-known *Letter from the Birmingham Jail*, "An injustice anywhere is a threat to justice everywhere." The increasing sense of members' identity with the Democratic Party has followed the deepening of this narrative through the coming together of factions, as many disparate marginalized groups have led the fight for equal rights and opportunity.

The experience of this discrimination by many who identify as party members has allowed the Democratic Party to make the claim that it is an advocate for equality and "the small guy" who lacks institutional support. This sentiment extends to economic policy as well as international concerns, as evidenced by the American-based anti-apartheid movement.

Taking the civil rights movement as our starting point, the camp of marginalized groups fighting for equality grew quickly. We saw this growth with the United Farmworkers and rise of the Chicano movement, which mirrored the strategy of the civil rights movement, and also looked for support among liberals and democrats. We saw it in the Asian American movement and development of ethnic studies programs on the West Coast. We saw it in the later waves of the women's movement and growing prominence of the movement for LGBT rights.

This theme of resisting injustice extends beyond specific marginalized groups. The environmental movement fights to keep the earth livable for all life-forms, not only today, but for future generations. The revitalization of the economic justice movement with the emergence of Occupy Wall Street fought for the 99 percent, and the Fight for $15 group is working to ensure that everyone in the United States is paid a living wage. We have seen it through antiwar activism demanding peace for the benefit of all involved parties. The list goes on. Liberal protest has the common theme of fighting for all forms of equality throughout its history.

These issues have not gone unnoticed by the Democratic Party. On the contrary, Democratic politicians have incorporated these causes in their rhetoric, and the Democratic Party has formalized the support of these issues in its party platforms. In doing so, the party has aligned itself in the minds of Americans with the work of the various activist movements pushing for legal recognition or protection for marginalized groups. When individuals identify with the work of any of these groups, they are more likely to identify as Democrats, and support party activity and candidates.

Both political parties have a history of attention to particular issues that convey their commitment to those points of public concern, thereby establishing the party's claim of ownership. In embracing their ownership of certain salient issues, the parties hope to convince voters that they are better able to resolve this public concern than other political parties (Rabinowitz and Macdonald 1989). Politicians' political campaigns reflect this issue ownership too, as candidates put out ads that draw on their parties' strengths and highlight the issues that have traditionally resonated with their bases. Political candidates running for office can rely on their political parties' positive history to boost their credibility and show that they are more competent than their opponent.

Though the parties tend to have ownership over different issues, traditional issue ownership by a specific party does not prevent opposing politicians from trespassing on a concern (Damore 2004). If the economy is doing especially well, governing Democrats may find themselves in a viable political environment to make the case that they are fiscally responsible, despite political criticism to the contrary. Yet even contemporary realities have to compete with long traditions of the parties behaving in a certain manner. Often it is the political traditions and trends of policy decisions that win out in the minds of voters.

Protests operate within this environment of issue ownership, and frequently deepen the association for voters between issue and party. When protesters make claims through their activism, they are criticizing the status quo. They present a problem that is facing the United States, and their protest actions demand that these challenges be reconciled. The question becomes who is best suited to address protesters' problems? If a political party has a reputation of consistently overspending, it is difficult to persuade voters that it would do an exemplary job managing the budget. When the electorate cares about the concerns voiced by protesters, voters examine the political credentials of politicians and their party to gauge their ability to handle the issue, which is why the party's historical behavior and priorities continue to remain relevant for voters. The more pressing the problem, the more political scrutiny current public servants and candidates running for election will face from the public. The reason for this is because voters are more concerned about problems that need to be fixed now, as opposed to future policy promises that candidates make during the campaign and hope to implement (Petrocik 1996). Protests can increase the importance of an issue for voters during an election cycle.[2] The party ownership of that issue becomes the foundation for voters' ideological classification of activists' grievances.

Formally Classifying Protest

As a consequence of this thought process and keeping the historical context in mind, I want to strengthen our understanding of ideological protest by bringing this concept to life with a tangible measure. To this end, I take a novel empirical approach that combines protest and issue ownership. I classify protest issues into *liberal* and *conservative* based on the party that has ownership over them. The first step in capturing the ideology of protesters is establishing an understanding of their message, which can come from multiple sources. I first rely on newspaper sources. I comb through newspaper accounts of protesters' grievances that have been reported in the *New York Times* and then classify these concerns into issue topics. At times the newspaper report on the protest will convey the protesters' message along with the goals that they were striving to achieve. Newspaper reports can also be incomplete, however, or the author of the article may simply not be aware of the nuances of the protesters' message. In these instances, I rely on related articles or even public information disseminated by the protesting organization, if such information exists. Once the message has been established, I take those messages and match them with the political party known to have ownership over this particular concern.

Now herein lies the rub of this process: *Which issues are owned by which parties*? In an effort to answer this, I identified whether liberal

---

2. Voters do cast ballots for the party they perceive as being most equipped to address the issue that they care about. This is not the case for every single issue but rather those that are most salient (Bélanger and Meguid 2008). Protest is often what makes these issues salient for voters.

or conservative politicians and citizens have largely supported the issue. To make this determination, I draw heavily on the extensive literature of issue ownership. A consensus has emerged from decades of study, and I pull from several established classifications of issue ownership (namely, Petrocik 1996; Petrocik, Benoit, and Hansen 2003–4.[3] The list of issues is too long to include here, but I provide a complete list in an online appendix. For each issue, I report the description of the claim made by protesters, followed by the ideological perspective that has largely owned that issue, and the reference citation that I used to classify the issue. To be thorough, I searched through several data sets housed in the Roper Center's iPOLL data bank, thus allowing me to identify specific questions and topics that were related to protest issues. I also report the average support of an issue broken down by liberal and conservative perspectives. The combination of previous authors' classification of issue ownership and public opinion polls drawn from several surveys as well as my own reading and interpretation of protesters' concerns allows for a suitable proxy of identifying the ideological position of protest grievances by issue ownership. Generally, the following are classified as liberal protest positions: civil rights expansion, feminism or women's rights, peace, international human and civil rights / democratization, environmental or green activism, pro-choice, and animal rights. The following are classified as conservative issue positions: pro-life, Christian right, anticrime, anti-immigrant/antiforeigner/ antiasylum, and anti-"transnational union."[4]

Across various issues, I incorporate more than a hundred unique claims expressed in political protest since the 1960s. The vast majority of claims can easily be classified as liberal concerns over which the Democratic Party has claimed ownership. Over time the Democratic Party has become susceptible to the influence of protests. This trend is partially due to the fact that the Democratic Party encompasses

3. See also Epp, Lovett, and Baumgartner 2014.
4. For a complete list of protest issues and whether they are coded as liberal or conservative, see the online appendix, "Appendix A: Classifying Ideological Protest."

many marginalized groups that are known to express their concerns through protest activism. These groups advocate particularly along the lines of identity. Over 90 percent of African Americans identify with the Democratic Party, followed by more than 60 percent of Latinos. The LGBT community also disproportionately supports the Democratic Party. For Democrats, protesting is one of the most utilized political tools to bring about change.

Protest issues do not always fit nicely in an ideological camp, and some protest events require us to observe other details about the event to determine the ideological underpinnings. For example, issues such as governmental functioning or corruption swing back and forth between the two dominant political parties depending on who is in office. Other issues are even more difficult to classify. As another illustration, it is not immediately apparent who has issue ownership over a protest advocating for healthy nutritional public school lunches. In a case like this, we might consider who is supporting the event, the demographics of the activists involved, or the targets of the protest event to determine the ideologies underlying the protest.

There are also protest issues that political parties do not want to be associated with publicly. The fact is, however, that parties are not always able to choose whether or not they own an issue. Rather, a combination of the party affiliation of the activists involved and perception of the electorate determines these associations. The Democratic Party of the early 1960s was very much associated with anti-black, prosegregation protests despite national efforts by the party to maintain distance. In the years after the passage of the 1964 Civil Rights Act, some of the racist components of the Democratic Party found a new home in the Republican Party. Few in the mainstream Republican Party would take ownership of the extremism voiced by white nationalists and white supremacists. Yet the post-2016 behavior of the Republican Party leadership in the face of the activities of white nationalists has left many voters questioning whether the party's efforts to denounce these groups go far enough.

This doubt arose prominently when white nationalist protests descended on Charlottesville, Virginia, in 2017. White nationalist protesters clashed with counterprotesters in the streets who gathered to oppose the anti-Semitism and bigotry on display. After the violence and bloodshed led to the death of thirty-two-year-old counterprotester Heather Heyer, Republican president Trump offered a false equivalency by stating there was "blame on both sides." This was despite the fact that it was a neo-Nazi who committed the murder that day by driving his car into the crowd. Trump also indicated that the members of the white nationalist protest group were "very fine people." It is possible that Trump was trying to appease a segment of his supporters given that the Ku Klux Klan official newspaper endorsed him in the 2016 elections and the former head of the Ku Klux Klan, David Duke, praised the efforts of his administration.

When white supremacists run for office, or offer political support and resources for candidates, they tend to do so with the Republican Party. Duke even served in the Louisiana House of Representatives as a Republican and identifies today as a Trump-supporting Republican. Regardless of the reason, it is clear that those advocating for white supremacy and joining white nationalist protest organizations see the Republican Party as an outlet to express their beliefs. The African American 2018 Democratic candidate for governor of Florida, Andrew Gillum, lobbed this claim against his opponent, Republican candidate Ron DeSantis, who had received support from neo-Nazi organizations. "Now, I'm not calling Mr. DeSantis a racist," Gillum began. "I'm simply saying the racists believe he's a racist" (quoted in Smiley and Flechas 2018). Gillum was making the point that even though Republican candidates might distance themselves from racist entities spouting hate in the public eye, these hate groups still see the Republican Party as a place where their message might resonate with some. For voters who witness protest groups spreading a message of hate and racism, it is less a question of who *owns* the issue and more a question of who *is closest to* it. Unfortunately, the Republican Party's recent history is more closely linked to this issue and thus has greater ownership than the Democratic Party.

Broadly speaking, individuals who run for office send signals of a party's character or association with an issue too. When it comes to race, voters see more minority political candidates running as

Democrats than as Republicans. Similarly, more women candidates run and put forth concerns related to women's rights on the Democratic ticket. The same can be said for "out" LGBT politicians. It is not a coincidence that the majority of minority, women, and queer politicians in the House of Representatives are members of the Democratic Party. When voters see individuals who embody marginalized groups and are more likely to advocate for liberal protest issues on the ballot for the Democrats, it further increases the tie between protest issues and partisanship over time.

Voters' perception of protest and ideology hold at both the national and local level. While considering national policies and candidates, though, the electorate's priorities are geographically concentrated; voters make decisions about national races with their local communities in mind. As discussed in the previous chapter, this means that local protests about national issues are more convincing than protests on the same issue occurring elsewhere in the country, even if those protests get more media coverage. After all, the electorate casts one presidential vote; everyone else on the ballot represents a local segment of the nation, whether that be state, county, or congressional district. Hence it is important to gauge protest along the lines that are most applicable and informative to the electorate. In order to capture the unique areas in which the electorate resides, we need to measure protest activism within fine-grained electoral boundaries.

Measuring and Mapping a History of Ideological Protests

After sorting protest issues along partisan lines, the most complex task still remains: measuring protest. This is difficult to accomplish because there is little consensus on how protests should be measured. I take several different approaches, coinciding with the question I am looking to answer in the chapters that follow and the availability of information on citizens' activism. Across these different approaches, I assemble local levels of protest across time. For our purposes, it is important to capture the location of protest activities over time because the geographic proximity to protest events could increase the probability that local citizens will be informed by activism (McVeigh, Myers, and Sikkink 2004, 680). Moreover, the timing of protest is important as protest issues may rise and fall given the political climate in which they are conducted.

To determine these parameters, my primary source of historical protest draws on reports of activism from the *New York Times* between 1960 and 1995 contained in the Dynamics of Collective Action (DCA) database and expanded with my own data collection efforts. This is arguably the most comprehensive source on national protest events. Newspaper accounts of protest are a "methodological staple" for studies of political protest (McAdam and Su 2002, 704). With the help of the DCA database, the *New York Times* has emerged as the most widely used newspaper source for analyzing the link between protest behavior and governmental action in quantitative studies.[5] The DCA database has been described in detail in a number of published articles and on the project's website.[6] Nevertheless, there are a few notable features of the data set that are worth mentioning in the context of our examination. First, the data came from reading *all daily* editions of the *New York Times* over the time period rather from using an index to locate candidate events (or simply coding the index to the *New York Times*). This is significant because this methodology reduces the biases associated with newspaper data (Earl et al. 2004). Second, newspaper articles were content coded by hand by trained coders to record information on many facets of each protest event (size, duration, tactics used, police action, and so on). This is important for our purposes because as I describe below, I wish to develop a measure of the *extent* of the informational cue sent by protests to an electoral district. Finally, the DCA includes protest events that occurred all over the United States and not just in a particular geographic region. This is noteworthy for my work

5. See, for example, Earl, Soule, and McCarthy 2003; King, Bentele, and Soule 2007; McAdam and Su 2002; Olzak and Soule 2009; Soule and Davenport 2009; Davenport, Soule, and Armstrong 2011.
6. http://www.stanford.edu/group/collectiveaction/cgi-bin/drupal/.

because I am interested in examining the effect of protest in electoral districts across the United States.[7]

I add to and transform the DCA data in two fundamental ways. First, from the information provided in the DCA data set, I place the more than twenty-three thousand protest events in their respective electoral districts. Second, instead of looking at a basic count of protest events, indicating simply whether or not a protest event occurred, I develop a measure to tap the scope or extent of the informational cue sent by protest events in a district in a given year.[8] I conceptualize the scope of information in protest in terms of levels of *salience* (Gillion 2013). Salient political protest is any protest activity that involves more than one hundred individuals, lasts more than a day, is supported by a political organization, results in property damage, draws a police presence, leads to an arrest, involves individuals carrying weapons, leads to injury, or involves death. I transfer the nine definitions given above into binary variables and then sum across the binary variables to calculate a saliency score for each instance of protest. Computed in this fashion, a given protest event can have a saliency score that ranges from zero to nine. To create a congressional district-level saliency score, for example, I take the protest events that occurred in a district for an election year and aggregate their level of salience.[9]

After creating an annual saliency score for each district, I then account for the ideological leaning, or *valence*, of the protest events in each district. To do this, I subtract the saliency scores of liberal

7. Although I rely heavily on the DCA database as a primary source for understanding electoral outcomes and historical trends of activism, I draw on additional sources of protest data to explore other aspects of electoral activity such as campaign contributions and voter turnout. These other protest sources are discussed in the chapters ahead.

8. To create a general measure of protest, I assess a wide range of citizen behavior that includes the following: demonstrations, rallies, marches, vigils, pickets, civil disobedience, information distribution, riots, strikes, and boycotts.

9. The saliency score is calculated as follows: yearly salience = $\sum_{i=1}^{N}$ level of salience, where N represents the total number of protest events in a congressional district over the course of a year.

protests from those of conservative protests in a district. In order to identify the grievance of protesters, and categorize protest events by whether they expressed liberal or conservative concerns, I borrow from several established classifications of issue ownership (drawn largely from Sigelman and Buell 2004; Petrocik 1996; Petrocik, Benoit, and Hansen 2003–4; Damore 2004). As a second form of robustness, I draw on several public opinion polls and calculated reports of citizens' favorability toward an issue based on their political leanings.

The final protest measure, then, is one that encompasses multiple aspects of protest activity. First, this measure builds on previous designs by encompassing aspects of protest that affect its ability to resonate with voters—that is, a measure of protest salience, as I discussed above. Viewed in this manner, protest can be conceived as falling along a continuum where higher scores indicate more informative events and scores that approach zero indicate less informative behavior. Second, this measure of protest captures the ideological leaning of the political signal interpreted by voters—that is, this is also a measure of ideological valence. When the measure is positive, the local political arena is dominated by protest activities that express liberal views; when it is negative, protests that advocate a conservative perspective have the louder voice. The result is a two-dimensional measure that can be placed along both the horizontal (ideological) and vertical (salience) axes. Finally, this measure is designed to echo the ways that voters perceive protest. Few voters rely on a single source of information, but rather are informed by multiple sources as well as perspectives. These various voices and perspectives influence voters in a holistic fashion; the sum total of protest events collectively offers voters a general understanding of their fellow citizens' concerns. In an effort to account for the combination of events that influence voters, my measure synthesizes information from multiple protests into a single general message. This message captures the intensity and valence of the overall ideological signal within each district that then influences electoral outcomes as people respond to this message at the polls.

We can apply this measure to any geographic region used to aggregate votes for a political position, including states (governor

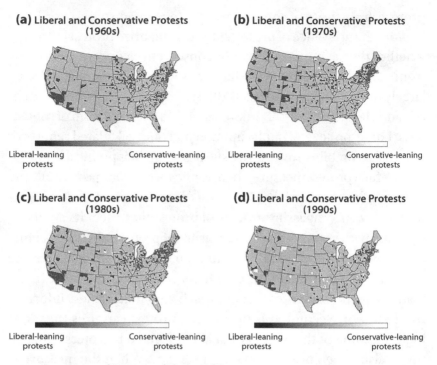

(a) Liberal and Conservative Protests
(1960s)

Liberal-leaning
protests

Conservative-leaning
protests

(b) Liberal and Conservative Protests
(1970s)

Liberal-leaning
protests

Conservative-leaning
protests

(c) Liberal and Conservative Protests
(1980s)

Liberal-leaning
protests

Conservative-leaning
protests

(d) Liberal and Conservative Protests
(1990s)

Liberal-leaning
protests

Conservative-leaning
protests

FIGURE 2.1. Geographic Layout of Ideological Protests

and senate races), counties (county commissioners races), school
districts (school superintendents), congressional districts (House
member races), cities (mayoral races), and even census blocks
(neighborhood watch committees). As an example, figure 2.1 graphi-
cally presents this measure by showing the location of liberal and
conservative protests by county. The darker shades, indicating liberal protest, dominate the map, and are initially concentrated in the
South and Northeast in the 1960s. Yet by the 1970s, liberal protests
are widespread. In addition to the variation of protest activities across
counties, there is considerable variation over time. Protests in the
1960s and 1970s largely expressed liberal views, driven by the civil
rights movement and anti–Vietnam War movements; 90 percent
of protests were liberal in both decades. The percentage of liberal
protests, however, dropped to 86 percent in the 1980s, and then to
78 percent in the 1990s, mirroring a similar trend of overall declining
protest activity.

While the overall frequency of protest has declined, the number of protests expressing conservative views has increased. Conservative protests began to emerge in a greater number of counties in the 1980s, with 14 percent of all protests expressing conservative values, up from 10 percent in the 1970s. By the 1990s, this percentage had increased to 22 percent. Protest events located in counties such as Teton, Wyoming, and Butler, Pennsylvania, shifted from predominantly expressing liberal issues in the 1980s to expressing conservative issues in the 1990s. This measure of protest fits nicely with historical accounts of citizen activism (see Soule and Earl 2005). What this visualization offers, though, is the ability to locate when and where competing concerns expressed in public protest began to shift ideologically.

Having measured and mapped out ideological protest, it becomes easier to see that this activism can set the agenda for political discourse and highlight salient issues for the American public. Local-level protests that occur in citizens' neighborhoods and towns amplify these concerns. If there is an abundance of protests happening throughout the nation as well as in local communities, this network of activism can bombard the political arena; the demonstrations may highlight issues that favor one party over the other by accentuating concerns that a particular party owns. Voters who live in areas with a large activist presence do become more aware of these wedge issues than those citizens who live in areas that see less political activism.

The Rise and Fall of Protest Movements, and the Ideology They Convey

Although some protesters may hope that the issues they are passionate about will be relevant in the eyes of the American public forever, the reality is that many protest issues become less relevant and other pressing concerns will ultimately overshadow them. The nature of protest growth underscores the evolving relevance of issues and their ability to elicit a public response. A protest can begin with just one or two incidents of citizens voicing their concerns and grievances in a public space. Yet these actions can grow in magnitude, swelling like a wave to lead to something much more. When these grievances are continuously expressed over a sustainable period of time, they form a movement.

Attempting to understand the rise and fall of these movements can be difficult for scholars because protests are fluid and activity can continue long after the height of a movement. Protest movements also often overlap with one another. In a nation with so many diverse communities, there are bound to be multiple groups simultaneously putting forth their concerns. Nevertheless, we can visualize the ebbs and flow of a particular movement by focusing on the level of protest. In figure 2.2, I place multiple protest movements alongside one another to demonstrate this variation over time, with light grey representing Democratic issue ownership and dark grey representing Republican issue ownership. Light Grey dominates the figure because protests on liberal issues have historically vastly outnumbered protests on conservative issues.

There were three issues that largely dominated the political arena in the 1960s. These issues were civil rights, pushback against the United Nations, and Communism. Following this period, a plethora of issues begin to emerge out of protest activities.

By the 1970s, a number of protest issues came from multiple movements, and their messages frequently overlapped with the narratives of other protest groups. For example, hundreds of thousands of individuals protested the war in Vietnam, yet the United Farmworkers' protests also increased the attention paid toward farmworkers' conditions and migrant rights. Education, anticrime, and women's rights movements also competed for the public's attention.

Protest activity was not nearly as widespread in the 1980s, though immigration protests emerged from both political sides. The nation was also concerned about international human rights. Antiapartheid protests denouncing segregation in South Africa spread across university campuses and found their way to Capitol Hill. The antiwar protests of the 1970s turned into protests against nuclear power. Despite many protest issues flatlining in the mid-1980s, by the end

Most salient issues of the messages in protests

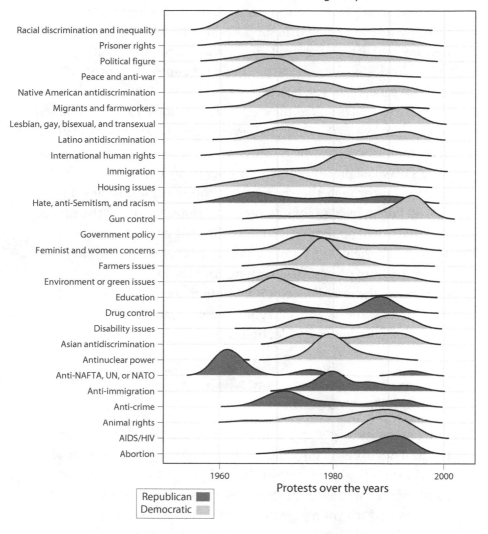

FIGURE 2.2. Issue Ownership and Party

of the decade, protest issues were back on the rise and some of the activism became notably contentious.

The 1990s saw the AIDS movement reach a crescendo with individuals protesting the lack of government efforts to bring awareness to HIV and AIDS. Often led by the group ACT UP, protesters engaged in civil disobedience, including chaining themselves to fences outside the Food and Drug Administration offices. Alongside the HIV/AIDS awareness movement was a burgeoning LGBT movement that started to mount multiple forms of activism. During this period, the movement saw its largest growth in support since the backlash that followed the 1969 raid of the Stonewall Inn, in which a police raid of a gay bar in New York City turned violent. The most contentious protest issue of the decade, however, was arguably abortion rights. Antiabortion activist extremists linked their cause to religious doctrine. Buoyed by this conviction, they bombed several clinics and caused the death of several clinical physicians. There were acrimonious clashes in the streets between protesters on both sides of the issue.

As seen through the shifting of protest topics, issues do not remain salient over an infinite period of time, no matter the degree of activism and public engagement. They rise and fall in importance as well as in the volume and frequency of events. Yet the rhythmic ebb and flow of protest issues, along with the longevity of activism, strengthens the overall ideological leanings that we cling to on a daily basis. Protest tracks with citizens' ideology and leads to a snowball effect that culminates on Election Day.

Strengthening Ideological Leaning through Partisanship

Can protest messages that convey an ideology strengthen citizens' political ties to one of the major political parties? It is not easy to alter individuals' allegiances toward "their" party. This identity is often fixed. Earlier studies of partisanship viewed it as an identity that was acquired at a young age through the influence of one's family of origin. Political identity was considered stable over the course of a person's lifetime and led to strong loyalty to one's party during their adulthood. This loyalty could only be shaken by "an event of extra ordinary intensity" (Campbell et al. 1960, 151). Later scholarship echoed these earlier works, and expanded the argument to propose that many short-term sociopolitical conditions have little effect on micropartisanship or individual changes in partisanship (Green and Palmquist 1990, 1994; Green, Palmquist, and Schickler 2002). A contrasting perspective of partisanship is found among scholars who study macropartisanship, the aggregate distribution of partisanship in the United States. These studies characterize party identification as being more fluid and susceptible to shifts in response to presidential popularity and economic factors (MacKuen, Erikson, and Stimson 1989; MacKuen et al. 1992; Weisberg and Smith 1991).

The fluidity in aggregate-level partisanship is seen through shifting electoral outcomes. Though voters have their mind made up by Election Day, the constant influx of information from political pundits in the media, campaign messaging efforts, and citizens' casual daily interactions with family and friends have shaped their decisions over the election cycle. In the lead up to the elections, there are tidbits of breaking news that might sway voters in one direction or the other. Crisis situations might also occur that make a politician's campaign and cause uniquely important for the current climate. At other times, prior incidents of impropriety might be unearthed to threaten, if not completely derail, a candidate's chances of winning the election. Any political candidate is vulnerable to the volatile response of an electorate that has been presented with shocking or salient information. The monitoring of voters' reaction to societal events through polling has become a hallmark of the way we follow elections and predict outcomes. The tracking of citizens' political attitudes about the elections in general indicates that voters are responsive to the changing world we live in. Protest activity can be an impetus for voters' perceptions, and harden their preexisting attitudes about policies, candidates, and parties.

The shifts in ideology that protests cause are rarely sufficient to bring about a complete party realignment for individuals where partisan voters would abandon the Democrat or Republican Party in favor of the other. Nevertheless, they do slightly shift party ties over time, even if only marginally. Even the most ardent scholarly supporters of partisanship stability allow for this possibility. Donald Green, Bradley Palmquist, and Eric Schickler (1998, 896) say that "identification with a party wanes somewhat when, year after year, it presides over hard times or lacks effective leadership." Indeed, changing political environments can lead to a political party's influence waning with citizens, but the party influence can also be strengthened by current events and prevailing sentiment. The issues voiced in protest contribute to these short-term fluctuations.

These protest issues resonate with citizens in different ways, and if the issues are salient enough for citizens, they can shift long-held partisan ties (Campbell et al. 1960; Carsey and Layman 2006). Ideological protests consist of multiple groups that allow voters to pose the question that Green, Palmquist, and Schickler (2002, 8) believe is pertinent for partisan ideology: "Which assemblage of groups (if any) best describes me?" When individuals become partisan, they are the most active in terms of helping their party in elections (Fowler and Kam 2007). Citizens use symbolic cues associated with various groups to influence their ideology and political affiliation (Conover and Feldman 1981, 642). For example, beneficiaries of liberal policies are often the ones to embrace liberal ideology (Conover and Feldman 1981).

Moreover, the underlying political divide that exists between conservatives and liberals is shaped by more than static differences in political ideology; it is also formed by the evolving political landscape as a whole (Zschirnt 2011, 685). Scholars have alluded to this link, arguing that when citizens can distinguish the party's differences on an issue, it is likely that policy positions will influence aggregate partisanship (Carmines and Stimson 1989; Macdonald and Rabinowitz 1987; Sundquist 1983). Being able to distinguish policy issues, however, often is not enough to strengthen or threaten ideological ties to parties. Citizens must also see these policy issues as salient topics for them to shape their partisanship (Carsey and Laymen 2006).

The attention that media outlets and academic scholars give to protest indicates that they do in fact view activism as highlighting salient issues—issues that these scholars and political pundits believe can shape outcomes just on Election Day. Political pundits seldom broach the specific topic of protest shifting partisanship strength over the entire course of the election. Yet the relationship still exists. Voting, for example, rarely occurs more than once a year. Is this the only time that protest is linked to political ideology? Of course not. Just like other tidbits of information that can derail or buttress a politician's campaign, protest messages are being divulged to American society on a regular basis, largely because protest is now happening daily. In some situations, there are multiple protests taking place on one day. Citizens are aware of this activism, and it is constantly shaping their political views.

Indeed, we need not wait for Election Day to see the relationship between protest activism and the embracing of a political ideology or partisanship. Throughout the year, protest can be connected to partisanship. We have to believe here that partisanship is not fixed. Polling evidence on partisanship indicates that it is not, and the proportion of Americans who align themselves strongly with one political party or another has been declining (Jones 2018). More specifically, polls conducted by Gallup have surveyed public opinion since 1935, and have inquired about partisanship and party identification since the 1950s. The data on partisanship over the years show a clear trend of individuals identifying less with the two national parties, especially the Democratic Party. There are also local trends occurring over just a month or quarter that reveal shifts in citizens embracing their political party, be it Democrat or Republican. Given that protest occurs on a daily basis, we can overlap the trends of party identification with protest activity to see how the two are connected.

Not all liberal voters identify with the Democratic Party, nor do all conservative voters identify with the Republican Party. The fastest-growing group of party identifiers actually includes those who consider themselves to be independent of political parties. In recent years, only roughly 35 percent of the nation identified as a party member for each party. Yet in every national presidential race, more than 50 percent of the nation supports one party's candidate. This shows that there are some voters who have a predisposition to an ideological leaning that matches up with a party, but choose not to identify with that party outside the voting booth. Ideological protests can influence these momentary partisan preferences in response to specific issues, even if voters' long-term party affiliation remains unaffected.

The important question at hand, however, is why might ideological protest lead individuals to become more partisan? Citizens view the party tied to the protesting activists through ideology as being the political entity that is best equipped to solve the grievances. This suggests that citizens are using their partisanship to synthesize their opinions on social issues on a daily basis. If an election was held on the same day that a significant liberal demonstration took place, liberal voters would overwhelmingly support the Democratic Party. The Republican Party would enjoy similar benefits for conservative protests. The essential point here is that the actual day of elections in November best captures the sentiment of voters at that moment. But if we could take a snapshot of voter sentiment throughout various points of time leading up to election and during the occurrence of protest, we may observe shifting partisan allegiances that reflect activism.

There is empirical evidence that citizens strengthen their partisanship during the same time that there are increases in ideological protests. Using Gallup poll data in table 2.1, I show the results of a regression model that directly captures the relationship between protests and shifts in party identification. The relationship is statistically significant and can be easily interpreted. When 10 percent of all protests in a quarter express conservative views, the number of those identifying with the Republican Party increases by 1.5 percent. This figure increases by 7.5 percent when 50 percent of all protests are conservative. Democrats fare even better when 50 percent of the protests are liberal, increasing those who identify with their party by 9 percent. In other words, the Gallup poll demonstrates that when liberal protest is on the rise, individuals are more likely to identify with the Democratic Party, and when conservative protest is on the rise, individuals are more likely to say they identify as Republicans. This captures the mood of the nation, and gives us evidence that waves of ideological protest overlap and correspond with individuals being more likely to embrace their ideological ties through party identification. These results suggest that protest makes appeals to the broader public, not just those most closely affected by the issues. The ideological segment of society that is sympathetic to this message embraces these appeals and supports the issue because citizens now see their political party as a vehicle to implement the change that they desire, thereby leading them to more closely identify with their party.

The causal mechanism that underlies the strengthening of party affiliations by protests is multifaceted. Although party loyalists

TABLE 2.1. Factors That Influence Partisanship

	Partisanship	
	Democratic Party (1)	Republican Party (2)
Ideological protest	0.0005***	−0.0004***
	(0.0001)	(0.0001)
Party of the president	−0.003	−0.011
	(0.009)	(0.009)
General election	0.007	−0.001
	(0.008)	(0.008)
Unemployment	0.009***	−0.002
	(0.002)	(0.002)
Party controlling the house	0.003	−0.012
	(0.018)	(0.018)
Periods of war	−0.067***	0.056***
	(0.010)	(0.010)
Observations	96	96
R^2	0.476	0.397
Adjusted R^2	0.440	0.356
F Statistic (df = 6; 89)	13.458***	9.746***

Note: *p < 0.1; **p < 0.05; ***p < 0.01

consistently vote along party lines and identify with a specific party, other citizens walk the line of partisanship, largely supporting a specific party and its candidates while still identifying as independent of the party system. Some of the shifts in party affiliations come from these nonidentifiers who become more emboldened to establish party ties as a way to address problems raised by political activists. Other support stems from those who truly are independent in terms of their identification as well as their ballot decisions. These individuals, too, can be persuaded by protest actions, as can newly minted voters. Support can even come from first-time voters who may have been spurred to participate and cast their first vote as a result of the protest activity's influence.

A voter's initial electoral experience, especially one that is motivated by protest activism, has the ability to guide entire future generations of voters down a certain partisan path. The contrasting party allegiances of Mexican and Cuban Americans capture this point. The two groups had vastly different political experiences on the way to improving the conditions of daily life. After Mexican Americans in the South endured the harsh vitriol of Jim Crow alongside African Americans, they adopted the strategies of the civil rights movement and applied them to their own Chicano movement to push back against job discrimination. Because the Chicano movement had many Democratic ties, the movement established a partisan political pathway for future generations of Mexican Americans to follow when engaging in politics. Cuban Americans did not have a similar protest movement. Instead, Cubans' introduction to the United States' political world came through the actions of President Ronald Reagan, who granted Cuban immigrants asylum. As a consequence, an older generation of Cuban Americans felt indebted to Reagan and became deeply entrenched in the Republican Party. Their introduction to politics in American society was through the actions of a conservative president rather than a tradition of liberal protest activity, and so their allegiances differed from Mexican Americans involved in the Chicano movement.

Partisan allegiances are important for electoral activity. The strength of citizens' party attachments shapes their reaction to national politics (Campbell et al. 1960, 128). Citizens are more likely to consider themselves members of a specific political party during contentious times in American history. The social and political tension of moments like this are compounded by protest messages awakening partisan attitudes. A negative consequence is that this can lead people to become narrow-minded and intolerant, making it harder to listen to those with different views (Huddy, Feldman, and Weber 2007). On the other hand, a huge benefit is that increased ideology leads to an increased readiness to respond to political cues from the in-group (Malka and Lelkes 2010).

Conclusion

Partisanship influences political preferences, and in return, political events shape partisanship. I have shown how partisanship is influenced by protest activity, but if partisanship is strengthened by activism, what does this mean for the electorate? Generally, partisanship will shape citizens' perception of the president's job performance, candidates' policy positions, and perceptions of issues (Bartels 2002; Johnston, Hagen, and Jamieson 2004). The relationship between partisanship and voting activity is even greater. Individuals who more closely identify with a political party will vote at a higher rate and engage in other electoral campaign activities more frequently (Abramson and Aldrich 1982; Brady, Verba, and Schlozman 1995; Campbell et al. 1960; Rosenstone and Hansen 1993). If we are to believe the strength of partisanship, then when ideological protest activity inspires stronger political ties to a party, that party will enjoy favorable electoral outcomes.

3

Political Primaries

PROTEST'S IDEOLOGICAL CONNECTION AT THE REPUBLICAN AND DEMOCRATIC NATIONAL CONVENTIONS

> But the engine is not connected to wheels, and so the "movement" doesn't move. Achieving that motion requires organizations capable of *old-fashioned* and permanent political work that can leverage street demonstrations into political change and policy reforms. In most cases, that means political parties.
> —MOISÉS NAÍM, "WHY STREET PROTESTS DON'T WORK," *ATLANTIC*, 2014

Political protests clearly play a function in the development as well as revision of law and government policy, but protest is often perceived as working on the edges of government. There are no formal institutional ties between protest movements and the government. When ordinary citizens have grievances, they simply head to the streets. They apply for permits to gather, spread the news about the event, and do so entirely independent of any governing body's oversight. Because of this independence, they have traditionally faced an uphill battle in having their concerns heard and acted on. The growing presence of protesters at national conventions may have transformed the ways that protest interacts with political institutions, however. Protesters are no longer engaging in random incidents of activism devoid of a political connection; they are increasingly finding themselves at the center of a political process that directly impacts electoral outcomes. One key way that protesters have begun to guarantee public officials are aware of their concerns is by demonstrating at the national conventions of the Democratic and Republican Parties. This choice of protest venue showcases the embedded political ideology of protests.

Indeed, political conventions mark one of the first points in the electoral cycle that we see the institutionalization of protest messages through an ideological lens. Protest during this early stage of the electoral process is closely connected to American political parties. It is *through* this interaction of party and protest message that ideological leanings in fact crystallize—that we start to see parties and, later, voters embrace or reject issues raised in protest. We can see protest as ideological through its role in facilitating shifts within the different ideological camps and its interaction with voters' perceptions.

This chapter connects protest to the early stages of the electoral process, and examines the link between protest and political institutions well before Election Day. In doing so, it considers the interconnected history of ideological protest and the national political convention, speaking to the history of conventions and how their purpose has evolved over time. The chapter tells the story of the first marriage between protest and institutionalized ideology at a national convention: the year when local Democratic Party leaders banned representatives from the Mississippi Freedom Democratic Party from attending the convention. The Mississippi Freedom Democratic Party was established by African Americans in Mississippi who felt disenfranchised from and pushed out of the voting process; its exclusion from the national party's convention highlighted the very reason that the group formed in the first place.

In many ways, protest reflects the prevailing topics of partisan banter found in the political parties' platform and messaging. When protests express party ideology, a reciprocal relationship forms between protests and the political party: activists provide salient messaging and grassroots mobilization that benefit candidates, while parties act as an institutional link between protesters' messages and the government's attention. This dynamic also means that candidates attempting to garner buy-in from voters must pay heed to protest movements and messaging.

Both voters and political candidates use the ideological leanings of protest to understand society. These messages are often relatable to those with a shared belief system. The coordinated and strategic activities of protesters at the 2016 Republican and Democratic National Conventions exemplifies activists' efforts to draw on these ideological leanings, buttress their message, and persuade the electorate to see issues from their perspective. But even more broadly beyond 2016, tactical protest efforts at national party conventions fortify the claim that political activism is inherently linked to a political ideology that is funneled into our American party system. As political conventions have become more public and open, protesters have seized on this opportunity to have their voice heard on a national stage. The political environment of the convention provides a natural experiment to study how protesters interact with convention attendees and party leaders—the most ideologically extreme components of the electorate. The interactions that protesters have with political parties are likely indicative of the strategies that they implement more broadly to persuade and convince voters. In this chapter, I take a closer look at what motivates protesters to engage in activism linked to the electoral process, how they interact with political parties, and how their ideology shapes their goals. In doing so, I seek to better understand protesters themselves in terms of what they want and what they hope to achieve.

Finally, protesters' activities at political conventions demonstrate an important tenet of the ideological protest framework: differing protest movements within the same ideology have overlapping concerns and goals. Voters have come to see protest activities as being linked to one another. When we walk among protesters asking them about their thoughts and opinions, it becomes apparent that a network of similar aims begins to form across the different groups, and that in turn later leads to the ideological ties that bind.

Revealing Protest Ideology and Political Strategies at the Convention

The link between protest and the behavior of the electorate consists of an abundance of moving parts, including volatile voting attitudes, voter turnout, and the character and policy positions of candidates running for office. While protests can send a message to the political establishment at any time during an election year, the parties' national conventions are particularly useful because protesters can interact directly with the individuals who have the power to set party agendas and goals. At conventions, the parties are refining their platforms, which then impact how candidates approach key debates leading up to the general election. This means that an effective protest at a national convention can influence the party leadership to change course on salient topics in ways that contestations at other venues cannot. Furthermore, the physical proximity of protesters to party officials also means party leaders cannot disregard the presence of protesters as easily as they might if merely hearing about the events on the news.

Protesters at the 1968 Democratic Party convention proclaimed that the "whole world is watching"—and it is: the world watches citizens' activism and movements' messaging when they protest at national party conventions. This public forum is reshaped into the hub of the public sphere where political deliberation is not verbalized but rather conveyed through creative poster signs and massive banners. Political activists use the spotlight of national conventions to court the media into drawing attention to the protest's cause and message. Some activists even refer to national conventions as the "next gigs on the concert tour," echoing the opportunity that conventions present to further momentum for their cause and engage in mass mobilization (Sobieraj 2011, 47).

In trying to capture the attention of the news media, however, protest organizations must be careful not to appear to be "insiders," blindly mimicking the party's platform, in their efforts to obtain legitimacy. These actions dampen their authenticity and decrease the coverage of their message by news outlets (Sobieraj 2010). Instead, activists must remain funnels of information that translate the convoluted pressing issues of the day into impassioned sound bites that resonate with the silent majority watching at home. They must do this by crafting compelling and relatable messaging that appears genuine.

Despite their efforts to be seen as outsiders, there are partisan sentiments lurking underneath the political activities of protesters. Protesters' partisanship identification shapes the potential structure of the coalitions that are formed between protest activists and party members, including party activists. We should be careful to draw a distinction between *protest* activists and *party* activists. Party activists are members of the political party who shape the nomination of political candidates, supply resources, determine rules of the party, and provide overall strength to the party organization (Carsey 2001). Party activists engage in institutional forms of political participation in order to have an impact in politics. Protest activists, on the other hand, are individuals in society who engage in extrainstitutional forms of participation, including protest behavior, to shape politics. Though protest activists are not always affiliated with any party, they have preferences and policy goals that are similar to party activists.

Protesters and party activists can both be classified as being either "pragmatists" or "purists." Pragmatic party activists care primarily about achieving electoral success for the party and the benefits that come with it, but purist party activists are driven by the issues and principles as well as policy positions held by the party (Wildavsky 1965). Protest activists have a similar distinction, where some champion electoral success over particular policy achievements. They throw their support behind one specific candidate and hope that this candidate not only wins the election but will also advocate for the issues that they care about once in office. This strategy assumes it is better to have a candidate from the protester's party regardless of the candidate's policy positions. It is a risky strategy because this type of protester does not make appeals to the other candidates; instead, all their attention and resources are focused on ensuring the success of their chosen candidate. Thus if the challenging candidate emerges victorious, the protester's issues are not likely to be incorporated into the new political agenda of the politician. Again, other protesters champion the issues and philosophy over loyalty to a specific candidate. They make appeals across the political aisle because they want their grievance addressed regardless of who is in office. They are also more concerned about their message being publicized (rather than protesting in order to influence the party leadership present at the convention) and persuading as many people as possible to see their perspective.

Over time, protesters have implemented both strategies in an effort to influence elections. Whether protesters narrow in on winning the election or supporting a specific issue, these strategies shape the link between activism and party. Most important, these protest strategies are publicly divulged at the party's national convention for the world to see, especially the silent majority.

The Interconnected History of Protests and Conventions as the World Watches

Understanding what national conventions are and how their function has evolved enables us to better consider how this element of the electoral process can institutionalize protest. The format of the national convention has changed significantly since its inception. When the first party conventions took place in the early 1830s in Baltimore, they were a necessary event because the political parties had grown to play a significant role in the electoral process. Initially, the convention was a formative part of an election process, in which political parties gathered to select the political candidate who would run on the party ticket. Before this process, candidates emerged through a caucus system that was riddled with problems.

Conventions served as a place to communicate party decisions to voters too. Party leaders would convene and reach a consensus on one candidate who would have the unified support of the party. It was not long before parties also began creating a unified message though a party platform. The parties hoped that their chosen political candidate would embrace this message during the campaign and eventually refer to these campaign messages as a set of guiding principles to lead the nation as president. But gone are the days when the convention served as a forum for delegates to publicly announce the presidential nominee after sitting behind closed doors and engaging in rigorous debate.

Today the nominee is known even before the convention begins, thus reducing this highly publicized convergence to an advertisement of party messages and showcase of the party's strength. Present-day Democratic and Republican National Conventions are billed as blockbuster events, attracting the Who's Who of the political parties, including top politicians, former presidents, and even future ones. These events often feature A-list actors giving speeches and celebrity artists performing music from their hit records, creating a festive, concert-like atmosphere. The conventions have become public spectacles in all their splendor. The cameras are on and rolling.

The path to the modern media coverage of the conventions began in 1924, when the Republican National Convention was broadcast live on radio from Cleveland. This would be the first time the public had a glimpse of the party's selection of its presidential candidate. The once closed-door conversations among delegates were now conducted in the open. This event was transformative for American politics and the electoral process. The novelty of the convention's radio broadcast piqued the interest of the American public and allowed people to follow the actions of the parties more closely than ever before. Public involvement in conventions would grow over time from interested observation to direct engagement.

The 1940 convention in Philadelphia was the first to be televised, but by the 1952 convention, the public was fully tuned in. Both party conventions were broadcast on television that year, more people owned TVs, and the coverage was widespread. The rise of the media, now a permanent fixture at conventions, opened the door for any newsworthy activity to be covered. This applied to both what was occurring inside the halls of the convention and what was taking place on the streets outside its doors. Conventions had been transformed from an insiders-only political event to an opportunity in the election cycle for protest activists to seize wide media coverage that they could leverage to spread their own messages as well as hopes for the party platform, policy, and electoral outcomes.

THE FIRST PROTEST CONVENTION

The Democratic National Convention of 1964 marked the first time a convention incorporated protest in such a way that it became intimately connected to the institutionalized ideology of a party. This first major incident of protest also unfortunately reflected the political times. Racism was alive and well. Although rampant across the Deep South, racism was particularly salient in Mississippi. African Americans experienced racism and discrimination in all aspects of Mississippi life, but none was more blatantly entangled with inequity than the process of voting in state elections. Black disenfranchisement in Mississippi went far beyond the voting booth and was seen even in the discriminatory practices of political parties.

The Mississippi Dixiecrats, or southern Democrats, blocked African Americans from voting using a variety of tactics involving intimidation and discrimination. This disenfranchisement should have rendered the primary election results invalid because the Dixiecrats had used an illegal discriminatory process to restrict the votes of black Mississippians—almost half the electorate. Yet the national Democratic Party considered the Mississippi Democratic Party's primary results to be valid and justified its delegates as legitimate.

Activists recognized the disenfranchisement of African Americans as an issue in need of immediate remedy and in 1961 formed the Council of Federated Organizations (COFO) to centralize various efforts of civil rights groups such as increasing voter registration. The council was an assemblage of some of the most well-known civil rights groups including the Student Nonviolent Coordinating Committee (SNCC), Congress of Racial Equality (CORE), and NAACP. In the summer of 1964, the Council of Federated Organizations held a separate election that was open to every person who met the requirements to vote in Mississippi. This vote was appropriately called the "freedom vote," and was a demonstration of black Mississippians' willingness to vote and engage in the political process. It also sent a defiant message to the Mississippi Democratic Party.

A few months later, the Mississippi *Freedom* Democratic Party (MFDP) was established. The "Freedom" in its name distinguished it from the Mississippi Democratic Party. The MFDP established a strong membership that consisted largely of African Americans, and incorporated the concerns and preferences of those who participated in the freedom votes. It held regular meetings, created a party platform, and hosted a state convention that produced sixty-eight delegates who planned to make their way to the 1964 Democratic National Convention and challenge the national Democratic Party to recognize them as party delegates. The MFDP, open to Mississippians of any race, served as the competing organization to the all-white Mississippi Democratic Party, which would not permit participation by African Americans. These MFDP delegates posed a challenge to the seating of the Mississippi Democratic Party at the convention in Atlantic City, New Jersey, advocating that their representatives should be seated instead of those of the Mississippi Democratic Party because of that state party's racially discriminatory practices. Hence the stage was set for confrontation at the 1964 Democratic National Convention, and political protesters would be at the center of this confrontation.

The 1964 Democratic National Convention marked the first attempt of liberal protest to influence a political party directly. The scene outside Boardwalk Hall in Atlantic City was unlike anything anyone had witnessed previously at a national convention. Thousands of protesters filled the boardwalk to make the case for the inclusion of the MFDP. The cause drew famous civil rights figures, who descended on the convention to highlight the crisis of voter disenfranchisement and uplift the MFDP's demand for recognition. Martin Luther King Jr. addressed the rally outside the convention hall right on the main boardwalk. He stood beside huge posters of the faces of three civil rights leaders who were murdered earlier in the summer in Neshoba

FIGURE 3.1. Black and White Protesters outside the 1964 Democratic National Convention Supporting the Mississippi Freedom Democratic Party.
Photographer: Warren K. Leffler

County, Mississippi. And he was not alone. Ella Baker, Bob Moses, and Stokely Carmichael were present as well.

While protesters rallied outside, direct political appeals were being made inside the hall. Activists worked to convince the Credentials Committee that the current Democrat Party had systematically hindered racial minorities from participating in elections through the use of intimidation and scare tactics. Though various individuals spoke indoors, no speech resonated like Fannie Lou Hamer's. Hamer talked solemnly about her experience. She told her heartrending tale of the day she tried to register to vote in 1962, when the owner of the plantation she had worked on for eighteen years told her, "We are not ready for that in Mississippi," and ordered her to leave that same night. She spoke of how after attending a voter registration workshop in 1963, en route back to Mississippi by bus, she was arrested, and then beaten and sexually assaulted in prison. As Hamer (1964) put it, "All of this is on account of we want to register and to become first class citizens and if the Freedom Democratic Party is not seated now I question, I question America."

Hamer later joined the protesters outside the convention, singing songs of hope and offering a few remarks. While apprehensive in advance of Hamer's speech, President Lyndon B. Johnson was moved by her actions. Walter Mondale, who served on the Credentials Committee at that time, said in an interview conducted much later that "Fannie Lou Hamer was more of a protest leader. She didn't seem to be interested in how we won the '64 election or how we kept our dignity, she just wanted change [a]nd she wanted it now" (Mondale and Ginther 2014, 108).

That year, the protesters did not ultimately get what they came for, and many associated with the MFDP returned to Mississippi disheartened. The Democratic Party offered the MFDP two "at-large" seats, leading to disagreement within the MFDP regarding how to respond. Yet even though the party did not succeed in securing representation for its delegates, the efforts of protesters at the convention spread national awareness about voter disenfranchisement generally and the oppressive practices of the Mississippi Democratic Party specifically. Individuals from all over the country began expressing their support for the MFDP. It is impossible to deny a connection between the increased salience of voter disenfranchisement caused by protest activity at the 1964 Democratic National Convention and the passage of the Voting Rights Act of 1965. Moreover, the national Democratic Party instated a new rule in advance of the next Democratic National Convention forbidding state-level Democratic Parties from discriminating on the basis of race.

At that next convention, in 1968, protesters again gathered at the national party conventions to air their grievances, in large part voicing disapproval of the United States' military action in Vietnam. Many activists were disappointed by President Johnson's efforts to keep troops in Vietnam. Even though Johnson had withdrawn from the race by the time the convention was held, the cameras were still present and the party leaders were still listening. The convention for the Democratic Party in Chicago became the classic example of citizens contentiously interacting with institutions of the electorate as a means of having their voices heard. While protesters are willing to cause a little mayhem to make their point, political parties work to keep their conventions as free of confrontation as possible (Troy 2016). These competing priorities met explosively at the 1968 Democratic National Convention. Although few remember the speeches that Hubert Humphrey, the party's eventual nominee, gave at the convention, many can recall the images of hundreds of protesters being arrested. The advent of television and its ability to amplify activists' messages at convention halls was not lost on the protesters. They capitalized on the opportunity for publicity. As protesters were carted away in police vans, they shouted, "The whole world is watching!" And it was.

The 1972 Republican National Convention in Miami Beach served as yet another opportunity for protesters to convey their message to the party leadership. Thousands of antiwar protesters converged on the convention, and hundreds of individuals were arrested as President Nixon was nominated for a second term. The GOP delegates attending the convention were welcomed with antiwar protests made up of various groups including the Black Panther Party.

By the 2004 Republican National Convention in New York City, convention-affiliated protest had grown throughout the nation until it became a staple of the party conventions. Convention organizers began to designate free speech zones in which to place activists. Local government and law enforcement tried to foster the perception that organizers were tolerant of protesters' activities—but some of these spaces were fenced-in pens. Though parties wanted to appear to value the input of the electorate, a competing concern when handling protest presence was to ensure as orderly a convention as possible. Even at a distance from the convention, however, protesters' grievances traveled far beyond free speech zones as their antiwar demonstrations made it on national news stations and forced political parties to speak about the government's efforts in Iraq.

The history of how protest found a home at political conventions is insightful. What is most intriguing about this political phenomenon is the congregating of multiple activist groups. Over the years, both the demographics of the protesters and the causes they support have diversified at conventions. What was once a couple hundred individuals protesting outside the building housing the convention grew to tens of thousands protesting across multiple blocks. The protests at conventions have spanned issues including the war in Iraq, global AIDS policy, poverty, racism, and education.

Modern Protests and Conventions: The 2016 Democrat and Republican National Conventions

We can learn a lot about protesters' approaches and strategies to sway voters by paying attention to their approaches to influence political party leaders and members. Given the protest activity at several electoral events during the political primaries, the 2016 Republican and Democratic Conventions provided an ideal environment to learn more about activists' tactics and motivations. Inspired by the history of protest influence at conventions and curious about the interworkings of ideological activism, I assembled a team of researchers to seize on this moment by conducting interviews with protesters at the Republican convention in Cleveland and the Democratic convention in Philadelphia. The information obtained from our efforts provided us the opportunity to more directly see what protesters' grievances were and witness firsthand how they expressed these concerns. We gained insight into what protesters are seeking to accomplish, who their targets are, and how they use the ideological vehicle of the political party—which it turns out, they do not use uniformly. The most important realization was that even though there were hundreds of protesters demanding change on more than a hundred different issues, they all used a similar liberal or conservative language to express their grievances to us. This network of responses highlighted the ideological unity that I have argued exists across protest activism. The final data set that was constructed from my research team's conversations now enables you, the reader, to in a sense walk among the protesters and be a fly on the wall while protesters interact with the party establishment.

DIFFERENT CONVENTIONS, DIFFERENT ISSUES, AND DIFFERENT GOALS

The 2016 Republican and Democratic conventions were different events, taking place in different parts of the United States, and supporting vastly different candidates. These differences attracted different protesters, with only minor similarities across the groups. In terms of demographics, protesters were overwhelmingly white Americans at both the Democratic and Republican National Conventions. There were also a disproportionate number of males protesting. Ideologically, however, we saw a different set of protesters engage in activism at the two national conventions.

The Democratic National Convention consisted of protesters who largely shared a liberal ideology and identified in some sense with the Democratic Party. Although over 40 percent of the protesters saw themselves as only weakly identifying with the Democratic Party, the vast majority of activists were situated somewhere squarely within the Democratic camp. Yet the groups of activists were not homogeneous, and a small percentage of protesters considered themselves to be truly independent. Even still, the ideological bent of protesters at the Democratic National Convention tended to be more liberal. At the Democratic National Convention, we were hard-pressed to find any activists who identified as members of the Republican Party.

Protests at the 2016 Republican National Convention tell a different story. There we found a greater diversity of opinions being voiced by protesters, often in direct competition with one another. This was reflected in the divergent allegiances expressed across protesters. As expected, there was a large percentage of individuals who identified with the Republican Party, and turned to protest as a way to persuade those who would set the party agenda and affect policy in much the same way that Democratic activists attempted to at the Democratic National Convention. Conservative protesters, however, were joined by a large number of liberal activists voicing competing concerns. In fact, there were more protesters standing outside the Republican National Convention who identified with the

Democratic Party than the Republican Party. These protesters considered themselves to be strong Democrats. Thus alongside Republican protesters advocating for their constitutional right to carry guns, for example, were Democratic protesters supporting gun control. Alongside the Christian conservative pro-lifers were liberal women activists rejecting the federal government's intrusion into their bodies. Given the competing ideologies and conflicting grievances of those protesting at the 2016 Republican National Convention, it is little wonder that this particular political event was more contentious than the 2016 Democratic National Convention.

Seeking to gain a clear understanding of the issues driving protesters' actions, we asked protesters what they considered to be the most important issues motivating their participation in the conventions. As we might expect, protesters at the Democratic National Convention offered very different responses than those given at the Republican National Convention.

During the Democratic National Convention, the two leading issues motivating protesters were disappointment over the party nominee and concerns about party corruption. In the minds of protesters, these two issues were linked. There was a fever pitch of outrage that emerged from the crowd. Many protesters were young activists who were upset that Bernie Sanders did not receive the nomination. They believed that something was amiss within the Democratic Party and a corrupt politician was at the helm. Protesters belted accusations of corruption about Hillary Clinton to anyone who would listen. And my team received an earful.

Though the country was reeling from racial tensions and contentious protest that had occurred in the months leading up to the convention, few people at the Democratic National Convention indicated that racism was a top concern. Actually, it was among the least concerning issues voiced by activists. But it may be too much to say that Democratic protesters did not care about race. Instead, the lack of protest around race was because activists did not see the Democratic convention as the best venue to address this specific concern. They voiced those concerns at the Republican National Convention—a place in which they felt that their message needed to be heard. There were actually more people of color, African Americans in particular, protesting at the Republican National Convention than at the Democratic National Convention.

Whereas only a few key issues were voiced among protesters at the Democratic National Convention, the Republican National Convention witnessed activists protesting about a host of different issues. Featured prominently among these were charges of racism and anger over the Republican Party's nominee for president, Trump. For protesters, Trump ran a campaign in which race was often in the background due to his rhetoric around immigration and his checkered past, which included questioning the citizenship of the first black president, taking out ads falsely accusing young black men of rape, and being charged with housing discrimination. Nevertheless, the issue of race was not the only topic brought to light by protesters. Protesters voiced additional concerns about issues like taxes and big government, religious liberty, LGBT rights, gun control, the economy, and abortion. These issues were rarely highlighted by activists at the Democratic National Convention, but were prominent at the Republican National Convention.

These were the issues that protesters cared about. Now they had to find the best strategy to bring those issues to the American public. My research team was able to discern the strategies of protesters by asking them about the goals they hoped to accomplish through this direct interaction with the electoral process. Similar to the wide variety of issues that protesters wanted to publicize, their goals differed across the conventions. These goals depended on the target of the protests. Protesters cared about changing public perceptions in ways that influence the electorate, the party hosting the convention, and the politicians running on the party ticket. The goals of protesters, however, differed by the ideology of activism and type of convention.

Figure 3.2 shows the distribution of liberal protesters' goals. The protesters' goals echoed some of the same issues and concerns that I discussed earlier. The goals of liberal protesters at the Democratic National Convention were largely driven by the desire to push back on the party nominee, Clinton. During the 2016 election season,

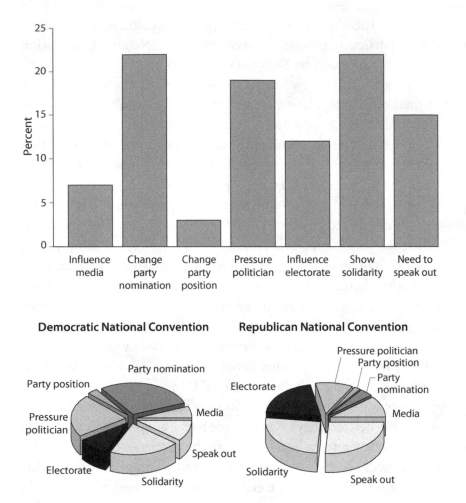

FIGURE 3.2. Liberal Protests' Goals and Targets

liberal protesters sent a stern message to the Democratic Party. They believed the system was corrupt and the elections were rigged. One protester, holding the American flag in his hand while yelling, "Stop corruption!" said, "The Democratic Party is broken. The Democracy of the US died and we turned the Democratic Party [in]to an oligarchy." The discontent was palpable. As a consequence, liberal protesters at the Democratic National Convention took the opportunity to try to improve the party's message and pressure politicians to appease their base. When liberal protesters descended on the

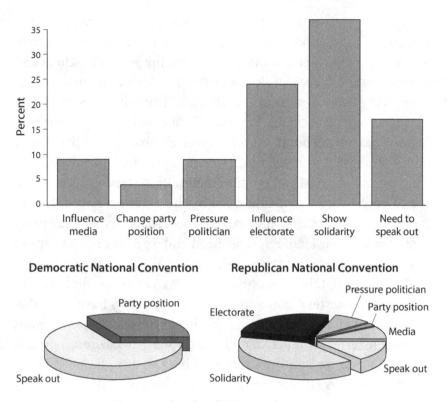

FIGURE 3.3. Conservative Protests' Goals and Targets

Republican National Convention, they looked to show solidarity with those who opposed the Republican Party, speak out against issues they stood for, and influence the electorate to vote against Republican candidates.

Conservative protests had a different set of goals when they interacted with conventions, as depicted in figure 3.3. At the Democratic National Convention, conservative protests were strictly interested in trying to change the party's position on issues and speaking out against the liberal policies championed at the convention. Conservative protests at the Republican National Convention, though, wanted to link to the party, and show solidarity for Trump and the Republican agenda.

While some of the strategies and goals of protesters for the 2016 Democratic and Republican National Conventions were specific to the general elections that year, other lessons are more generaliz-able. It is clear that protesters do care about reaching the electorate and influencing voters. In many incidents, the goal of reaching and persuading the American electorate overshadows other priorities of influencing political parties. This offers evidence of protesters' belief that their work does change minds and influence the choices that vot-ers will make in the booth. Another generalizable point is that liberal and conservative protests at each convention differ beyond ideologi-cal position on social and political issues. Protesters' goals to shape the electorate are also conditioned by the party they are trying to target. Broadly speaking, they express more solidarity with the party that mirrors their ideological position and a greater need to speak out at those conventions that are hosted by the party they oppose.

The biggest takeaway, however, was yet to be discovered. Although protesters' issues and goals could easily have been dis-cerned through activists' comments while the research team was out in the field, a deeper understanding of the link across protest groups would have to wait until we returned back to our offices and ana-lyzed the data. We discovered that in the midst of all the differences we found at the conventions, there emerged a unifying ideological strand that connected the various protest movements.

A NETWORK OF PROTEST: THE IDEOLOGICAL CONNECTION IN PROTEST

While engaging with protesters, one of our first steps was to identify the different protest movements that were present at the national conventions and their concerns. To this end, we asked about indi-viduals' association to groups and their support for the political causes we believed they were attempting to address with their pro-test activity at the time. We later used that information to classify the protest movement to which that individual belonged. We also asked individuals to freely state why they were protesting and what they considered to be the most important issues facing America. Because these questions were open ended, individuals could say whatever they wanted. My approach to surveying protesters at the convention with an unstructured format was intentional. It allowed us to acquire more context behind protesters' actions. In some cases, letting respondents talk freely led individuals to discuss every single ill that plagues American society. In other cases, individuals were hesitant and even afraid to say much or speak with us at all. Nevertheless, the typical protester had something to say and was willing to share that something with anyone who would listen.

Our conversations with protesters highlighted ideological protests in fascinating fashion. In figure 3.4, I plot a network of the reasons that individuals were protesting and the various movements to which they belong. The slightly bolded and encircled words represent the different protest groups present at the convention. The lines coming out of those protest groups—lines connecting to smaller words and phrases—represent summarized responses and specific statements that protesters used to express their grievances.

The network in figure 3.4 captures two important points. First, protesters from different movements have overlapping grievances that they want to address. For example, income inequality was a concern expressed by individuals who came from the women's movement and those protesting low wages. As another illustration, a "lack of God" was a concern that connected individuals who associated themselves with proreligion protest to those who viewed themselves as protesting taxes. Overlapping grievances move far beyond what we would expect, such as issues of corruption and big money in politics, health care, racism, sexism, and others. These overlapping issues do suggest that there is something in common with different protest movements. The commonality connecting these groups, as I argued earlier, is ideology.

The second and crucial observation captured by figure 3.4 is the way overlapping grievances fall along ideological lines of issue ownership for the different political parties. There is a large cluster of protest events in the center of the picture, capturing movements of liberal protest that include environmental issues, proimmigration, gun control, and so on. The Democratic Party is supportive of these concerns. Conservative protests supported by

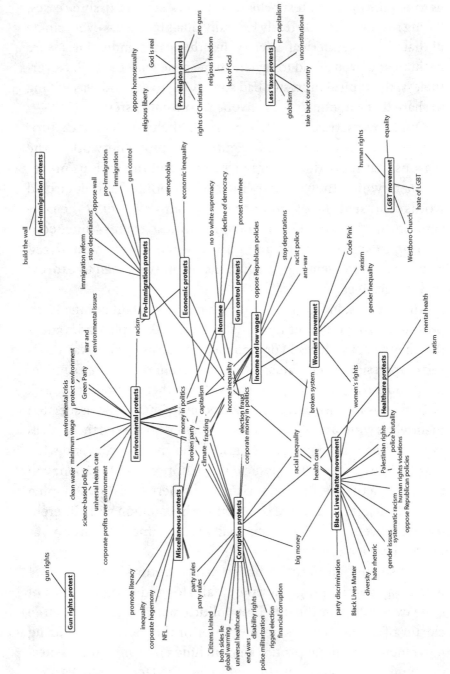

FIGURE 3.4. Network of Movements

Republicans such as gun rights, anti-immigration, and proreligion protest, on the other hand, hover on the edges of the liberal nucleus center. These protest groups do link up with one another, but to a lesser extent than liberal protests. Indeed, our earlier theoretical notion of these movements possessing a unified ideological voice is borne out on the steps of the Republican and Democratic National Conventions.

Conclusion: The Bird's-Eye View of Protest, National Conventions, and Political Ideology

In this chapter, I examined the ways that protest interacts with political parties and ideology at the Democratic and Republican National Conventions. This interaction continues to take place throughout the year before later materializing into substantive electoral gains. Protest at conventions takes advantage of press coverage to optimize the reach of the protest message to the electorate and attempts to draw party leadership attention to the protesters' priorities. The Democratic and Republican National Conventions provide a platform for protesters to amplify their messages to voters who are cognizant of the national conventions. Protest messages do also shape the perceptions of candidates moving forward, as they continue to analyze the political leanings of their current or potential constituents as well as understand their political fortunes. While activity at the conventions is geared toward presidential candidates, other political candidates observe the positions that protesters are putting forth. This may shape the way in which they campaign and lobby, since protest issues foreshadow what voters consider to be important.

The convention is an opportunity to observe where the parties stand in relation to where activists stand. While unable to capture the whole picture, our interview data are helpful in allowing us to witness the dance between protesters and ideology, exemplified by the political parties and on full display at the national conventions. Rather than highlight the specific stories of individual protesters, for the purposes here it is more useful to consider the patterns that emerge across them. Ultimately, this work is concerned with protests' impact, and I accordingly place the weight of my attention on the people who receive protest messages. Hence I focus on how receptive voters might be to a message rather than speaking about the specific ways in which protest changes campaign narratives.

What we see at conventions, and what I will explore up to Election Day in subsequent chapters, corresponds to my theory that a unifying ideological message connects multiple protests and movements. This ideological message serves as the bond, or an ideological bridge, that resonates with the electorate. This applies equally to liberal and conservative protest; it just happens that protest is a political tool utilized more by liberal populations. At the national conventions, protest messages are being funneled through the two-party system, synthesized and digested in a way that voters can understand, and later recalled as people make decisions in the voting booth. Protesters may not share specific policy goals—certain folks may, for instance, want to focus their protest message on gender, race, or religion—but when we step back from the minutia of topics, we can see that the overall mood of the nation is changing. As I will explore next, this shift in mood is related to protest and has an important impact on campaign dollars.

4

Campaign Contributions

FOLLOWING THE MONEY TO FIND THE FINANCIAL BENEFITS OF PROTEST

The night after the election was the first real protest any of us had been to. I was driving my daughter to dance class and she had a friend in the car and we heard on the radio that there was a protest downtown. They were like, "Mom, can we go?" and I was like, "Absolutely." I turned the car around and we went downtown and just marched with everybody and screamed obscenities and it was pretty awesome to see the girls get so involved. They felt empowered. So that sort of became our thing.

—KATE FRICKE, PORTLAND PROTESTOR SPEAKING WITH THE *OREGONIAN*, 2017

Citizens with ample discretionary income find many of their most meaningful instances of legislative representation through what one might call "monetary surrogacy."

—JANE MANSBRIDGE, "RETHINKING REPRESENTATION," 2003

Money and politics have become inextricably intertwined. Multimillion-dollar corporations lobby politicians with the hope that they can influence policy in ways that will benefit their shareholders and increase profit margins. Interest groups, from the Left and Right, also pour millions of dollars into the pockets of politicians with an eye toward raising their priorities on the policy agenda. But the big money in politics does not stem from greedy corporations or self-serving interest groups. No. The real big money comes from the American people in the form of campaign contributions. Over the 2016 election cycle, citizens poured $600 million into politicians' campaigns with their individual contributions.[1] The amount of money citizens donate to campaigns has risen over time and is expected to go even higher in upcoming elections.

Supporting candidates through campaign contributions is the first opportunity individuals have to formally engage in elections. Individuals are not making campaign donations out of a sense of altruism. They are prompted to give, sometimes as a result of a specific request or propelled by their lived experience. Frequently, though, the individual act of giving to a political campaign is just as ideological and partisan as the act of voting. Because of this, ideological and partisan events can potentially mobilize giving. Ideological protest is one such event that could provide the impetus individuals need to give to politicians' campaigns, especially if these salient protest actions are actively occurring in voters' backyards.

Many do not think of protest as being a moneymaking endeavor. This chapter, however, asks that specific question: Is protest profitable? The mere suggestion of protest profitability might not sit well with activists. After all, as we saw in chapter 3, many protesters engage in massive demonstrations *against* the involvement of money in politics. Even though protesters may not participate in protests in order to generate political financing, they may unknowingly be one of the greatest forces that brings money into politics. This is yet another way that protest ultimately shapes electoral outcomes.

---

1. Individuals also gave $1.05 billion to large political action committees, which raise and spend money (Rosenberg et al. 2017).

In this part of the book, I set out to explore the world of campaign contributions made during the 2018 midterm election cycle. In doing so, I take a microscopic view of two intriguing areas with a surprisingly significant level of political protest: Portland, Oregon, and Phoenix, Arizona. These two locations experienced unprecedented protests that were strongly associated with an increase in political donations—a somewhat-unusual occurrence for these cities. After examining these fascinating cases, I take a step back to look at campaign contributions across the entire country and map political donations to ideological protest taking place within local neighborhoods. As we will see, political donations reveal the first impacts of ideological protest. For some politicians, protest becomes the gift that keeps on giving.

The Meaning of Giving and Why We Do It

Regulations around political giving have fluctuated over the decades, largely because giving to a political campaign is considered by some to be an act of speech. Legal scholars have debated the correct interpretation of spending and the appropriate classification of giving that the government should use to regulate campaign contributions. If campaign donations are purely acts of speech, then they should be treated as a First Amendment right and subsequently afforded more liberty from government oversight. If they are something *similar* to speech, but not actually classified *as* speech, the government should, legally, have greater control over donations. Though this classification has shifted over time, the Supreme Court has set the tone for how campaign giving should be viewed.

In the wake of congressional reactions to Watergate, which led to the House and Senate limiting campaign contributions and individual expenditures with the 1974 Federal Election Campaign Act, the Supreme Court indicated that campaign contributions were forms of political speech in the 1976 ruling in *Buckley v. Valeo*. Critics who push back against the Supreme Court's wisdom argue that money is not purely speech because it does not communicate ideas (Wright 1976, 1019). Deborah Hellman's (2013, 953) crafty saying encapsulates the tension between the perspectives: "money talks but it ain't speech." Hellman's statement, I believe, gets it right. Giving might not be speech, but it surely talks; it says something about how citizens view the world and communicates their political preferences. Making donations to specific campaigns and causes is also directional, and indicates people's allegiances.

Campaign contributions are investments that corporations, interest groups, and individuals make in attempts to influence political outcomes. The return on this investment can sometimes be negligible, especially if a contributor's expectation is to swing an election. Still, these contributions do achieve the political goal of shaping policy. In the sugar industry, for example, special interest contributions were consequential to policy outcomes for the 1985 agriculture bill. Economist Thomas Stratmann (1991, 615) writes about the bill's passage that a "$3000 sugar PAC contribution maps into a 'yes' vote with almost certainty." In looking at the banking industry, he found that a $10,000 contribution raises the probability that congressional members support banking legislation by 8 percent (Stratmann 2002, 361). For instance, when financial services legislation was up for consideration in 1991 and 1998, congressional members changed their votes to support financial bills in response to the level of campaign contributions they received, with Republicans being more responsive to such donations than Democrats (Stratmann 2002, 360). Voters might not know how much they have to give to make the difference, but they generally believe that their dollars move them closer to their preferred policy outcomes.

But who are these donors, and why are they giving? If it is the case that money talks, then one issue with campaign contributions is that people who have greater financial resources are able to speak louder than others. Critics of the classification of political donations as speech point to the inequity this creates due to the large differences in citizens' and corporations' capacities to give. The wealthy gain disproportionate influence because they can give more. In fact, giving has come to be seen as the source of political inequality to such a point that many believe that money in politics has corrupted our democracy (Alexander 2003; Kuhner 2014).

It is true that wealthier individuals, who possess greater discretionary income to give, drive campaign donations—and because the "überwealthy" in this country (those who find themselves in the top 1 percent) tend to hold more conservative views, campaign funding from this source benefits the parties unequally.[2] And these überwealthy individuals are extremely politically active (Page, Bartels, and Seawright 2013). They are particularly active with campaign contributions.

While giving has historically been a political activity of the wealthy and big corporations, average voters have started to use their dollars to aid political campaigns. The influx of contributions from average donors in the electorate typically comes in small donations of $200 or less. President Barack Obama's election campaign is a great example of this point because he was a major benefactor of small donors. In 2011, Obama raised $56.7 million by way of small donations. This fund-raising achievement was unprecedented for small donors. The achievement also bested the previous record for small donor contributions set in 2008–a record that the Obama campaign also attained. President Obama's small donations in 2011 amounted to more than the total amount that his competitor, Mitt Romney, raised from all his sources (Malbin 2012).[3]

There are several reasons that voters may contribute to a campaign if they have the financial resources to do so. The local political environment plays a large part in shaping when, how, and to whom citizens make campaign contributions. This is in part because individuals' communities serve as networks of social influences that encourage giving (Brady, Schlozman, and Verba 1999). Scholars note that there is something about the local environment that impacts giving. As James Gimpel, Frances Lee, and Joshua Kaminski (2006)

2. The conservative political views of the most affluent, in part, are nurtured through the socialization process at the affluent colleges they typically attend (Mendelberg, McCabe, and Thal 2016).

3. The nice benefit of small donors is that they can give on multiple occasions. This is simply due to the fact that they will not hit the $2,700 limit with one contribution. Political parties are aware of this untapped potential and constantly solicit support from voters throughout the election cycle.

correctly conclude, the campaign contributions of your neighbors influence the amount you give. Yet explanations of this local-level influence have been vague, and scholars struggle to put their finger on the underlying mechanism that motivates giving in a local community. Though the reason remains a mystery, your neighbors can clearly shape how you give.

The most straightforward explanation for why individuals donate to campaigns is because they are asked to do so. Individuals give particularly to local parties after they have received personal requests for donations (Brown, Powell, and Wilcox 1995; Grant and Rudolph 2002). Once voters give, they will likely become part of a core group of "habitual givers" who contribute in every election cycle, especially for presidential campaigns (Brown, Powell, and Wilcox 1995, 30).

I cannot help but wonder if there is more to the story of campaign contributions than what the current literature has unearthed. Sure, we know a lot about who gives money, but we still struggle to identify why. Apart from a wealthy, politically active local environment and being asked for donations personally, we know little about the underlying motivator that provokes individuals to give. I argue that an important factor that has been overlooked when attempting to explain why voters contribute to political campaigns is ideological protest.

Why Protests Are Moneymaking Endeavors for Political Campaigns

Local protests work to influence campaign contributions on two fronts. First, political activism provides a source of mobilization for citizens' engagement generally. Those who are closest to the protests are more likely to be aware of and interested in the issue that activists are addressing because it affects them directly. These informational cues can heighten political interest and make local citizens ideal donors. Political interest in and knowledge of an issue can even be powerful enough to overshadow the consideration of the financial resources that citizens actually have to give to a party (Grant and Rudolph 2002). While the entire nation may be aware of a given protest taking place in a specific area, those who are closest in proximity to it are more likely to be swayed to political action.

On the second front, ideological protest at the local level offers some sense of directionality for what type of candidate citizens should support. Citizens give to obtain personal benefits that can come in the form of material gains, but donations can also be a way to express solidarity with individuals aiding like-minded politicians (Wilson 1973). Similarly, interest groups are more likely to donate money to candidates who share their ideology (Poole and Romer 1985, 65). In this atmosphere, ideological protests provide a guiding light for how individuals should give. They highlight the importance of an issue as well as sound the alarm of urgency for voters to support Democratic candidates during liberal protests and Republican politicians amid periods of heightened conservative protest. These ideological protests also strengthen the link between voters and their preferred candidates. When candidates have strong ideological connections to contributors, the chances of soliciting donations through less traditionally successful means, such as direct mail and telemarketing, increases (Brown, Powell, and Wilcox 1995).

Although local protest is especially effective in motivating individuals to become involved in politics, citizens' financial support does not necessarily go to the politicians who represent the area in which protest occurs. As a matter of fact, political candidates often receive the bulk of their campaign contributions from citizens who do not reside in their district—by a margin of two to one (Gimpel, Lee, and Pearson-Merkowitz 2008). Political protest spurs giving that can be directed to any political candidate who citizens see advocating for the ideological positions expressed by protesters. A shared ideological link between citizens and political campaigns is a strong impetus for individuals to donate to particular candidates (Barber, Canes-Wrone, and Thrower 2016). This link can move beyond the geographic confines of a congressional district and be shared with protesters from miles away.

Further, to elicit donations, candidates' positions do not need to match the ideology of campaign donors issue for issue. This is where the party of a political candidate becomes influential, serving as an ideological calling card for the voting public. Liberal voters, inspired by liberal protests, anticipate that their dollars will be better spent on Democratic politicians; Democrats are perceived to be more credible than Republicans when addressing the liberal issues voiced by demonstrators. The same can be said of conservative protest and Republic politicians. It is no wonder that once individuals have been mobilized to give, they tend to give to those individuals whom they trust to advocate for their concerns (Francia et al. 2003).

Although protests' ties to campaign dollars might be a foreign concept to some, protest has a proven track record of shaping spending in the United States. Protests are known to impact the flow of money in the corporate sector. Protest activism can impact firms' investments (Soule 2009). Protest also influences companies' stock shares, especially when those companies cater to critical stakeholders such as labor unions and consumers (King and Soule 2007). In these ways, protest can shape the financial performance of businesses as well as their policies and practices (for a review of firms, see Soule 2018).

The American public relies on political activism to become informed of any hostility toward a company's business endeavors. Consumers may then use their personal dollars to support or boycott a company's products. Thus when a protest takes place, a company's reputation can be damaged as a result. Political figures monitor this intricate dance among protesters, citizens, and business firms. The flow of money becomes political as politicians distance themselves from corporations that suffer reputational damage inflicted by activist movements (McDonnell and Werner 2016). Politicians are even inclined to refund campaign donations to corporations that have experienced boycotts as a way to distance themselves from the company's controversy, and align with the priorities of the protesters and sympathetic members of the public (McDonnell and Werner 2016).

Just as politicians distance themselves from problematic corporations, companies recognize the political nature of money and distance themselves from politicians who would be bad for business. For example, several companies requested that their donations be refunded in the midst of a public backlash when Mississippi senator

Cindy Hyde-Smith proudly proclaimed that she would attend a "public hanging" if invited and would be "on the front row." Spoken in a state with a dark past of lynchings and hangings, the public hanging reference harked back to slavery and the years afterward, when racist communities in the South would come together to joyfully watch African Americans being hung by a rope, dropped a few feet to suffer a gruesome death from strangulation or a snapped neck. Although Senator Hyde-Smith exuded a sense of pride for this horrific tradition, her words were met with several protests. In light of her comments and persuaded by the public outcry, major corporations that had previously contributed to Hyde-Smith such as Google ($5,000), Facebook ($2,500), and the MLB ($5,000) requested that she return their campaign contributions.

Protests, however, are often money-generating events that raise funds from average citizens. With the rise of crowdfunding options such as CrowdJustice, CrowdPAC, and GoFundMe, giving has become nearly effortless. Donations can be given online, at your own convenience, and behind the veil of anonymity. As a consequence, protesters have been able to mobilize average citizens to contribute large sums of money as well as small donations toward their causes. Protesters' efforts have sparked financial support that sums to hundreds of millions of dollars.

GoFundMe, a leading platform for grassroots fund-raising, tracks citizens' donations and demonstrates the money-generating power of protests. Among GoFundMe's extensive database of public giving, there are several examples of veterans' protests, including their involvement against the building of the Dakota Access Pipeline. The pipeline would go through a Native American reservation and potentially taint the area's clean water supply in South Dakota. The 2016 "Standing Rock" protest garnered $1.1 million to support the efforts of continued activism against the pipeline. The official Sacred Stone Camp GoFundMe campaign, also designated to support the efforts of protesters, provided an additional $3.3 million to the activists.

The organizers of the March for Our Lives campaign in the wake of the Parkland shooting, in which a nineteen-year-old expelled student murdered seventeen students and staff members at Marjory Stoneman Douglas High School, raised an incredible $3.6 million to help organize protests throughout the country and beyond on March 24, 2018.[4] The Democratic Party even seized on earlier protest events that occurred in February of the same year to increase its monetary resources. It made the already-ideological protests more partisan by blaming the Republicans in office for failing to enact laws that could have prevented the shooting while asking for voters' dollars through a massive email campaign that read in part:

> Inspired by the students in Parkland, Florida, people nationwide are coming together to bring an end to gun violence. Just this week, survivors of the Parkland shooting confronted lawmakers at the Florida state legislature and made their voices heard, and thousands of people gathered to support them. . . . Show you're in to stop the cycle of gun violence. Donate $3 before Wednesday's deadline and together we will defeat Republicans who want to maintain the terrible status quo. (Mosley 2018)

Even journalists covering protests have secured money to support their reporting through GoFundMe. An independent news outlet called Truthdig (2018) raised an astonishing $21,000 simply to provide "in-depth, on-the-ground reporting and exclusive multimedia coverage" of the Poor People's Campaign. The protest event was a forty-day campaign launched in May 2018 to revitalize King's call to end income inequality, and reporting on it was profitable.

In sum, protest is a multibillion-dollar enterprise spread throughout various sectors of American society. Some of that funding ends up in the political arena to support political candidates' campaigns. This indeed was the case for Portland and Phoenix during the 2016 to 2018 midterm election campaign.

---

4. This amount is separate from the Stoneman Douglas Victims' Fund that raised $10.1 million, which was allocated to provide relief and financial support to victims.

Large Protests and Big Money: A Case Study of Portland, Oregon, and Phoenix, Arizona

If we think about the geographic areas that could be considered hubs of liberal protests, we are likely to name major metropolitan areas such as New York City, Los Angeles, Chicago, Washington, DC, and various areas in the South. We typically do not consider Portland or Phoenix, or their surrounding areas, to be epicenters of protests in America. These areas did not play a dominant role in some of the most historic movements in the United States, including the civil rights, women's rights, and LGBT rights movements. Yet in the weeks following Trump's 2016 election, these areas became a powerful voice for liberal change. And this change would become connected to financial gains for candidates within the Democratic Party.

In many respects, Oregon and Arizona are quite different from one another. Oregon is a more liberal state than Arizona, both in terms of its representatives and electorate. The physical climate of Arizona is significantly warmer than that of Oregon. The geographic location of Oregon puts it close to the Canadian border while Arizona sits on the Mexican border. And the college football teams of Oregon are better than Arizona's, subjectively speaking. These differences, among others, set Oregon apart from Arizona. Nevertheless, between the 2016 and 2018 election cycles, the levels of liberal protest activity were almost identical.

The protests in Phoenix were largely liberal throughout the midterm election cycle. Individuals were upset after the 2016 elections and vented their frustrations in the street. Activists' ire, however, turned directly toward the Republican mouthpiece, Trump, after the race-based violence in Charlottesville. Trump's first rally following Charlottesville happened to be in Phoenix, and he was welcomed by fierce protest events.

Liberal protest in Phoenix continued to mount from there. High school students marched out of classes across the city in a protest over a lack of gun control legislation that would keep them safe. In one notable action at Hamilton High School, students walked out of class and onto the track field. The crowd of hundreds of students linked their bodies together to form a massive "SOS"—the universal sign requesting help when in extreme distress—that could be seen from an aerial view. Students also held a "die-in" at the capitol to demand change in gun control policy. These protests were in solidarity with the thousands of students protesting in Florida after the tragic shootings at Douglas High School.

Student protests over gun control were not the only ones stemming from Arizona schools. Public school teachers in Phoenix as well as other parts of Arizona went on strike to protest their low pay. Their median salaries of $42,000 across the state placed them at forty-ninth in the nation for teachers' pay (Cano and Gardiner 2018). This inequity garnered teachers' activism.

In Portland, protests were also ignited by the liberal pushback against Trump's presidential election. The largest liberal protest in Portland was the Women's March that took place in January 2017, immediately following Trump's inauguration. The timing of the event on the first day that Trump took office was purposeful. It was a reaction to all the controversies that arose during this presidential campaign—from the video that featured him bragging about grabbing women's genitalia to the generally disrespectful comments he made about certain women. The protest event in Portland drew more than seventy thousand activists, with local newspaper outlets calling it the largest public demonstration in Oregon's history. While the protest was coordinated by women's movement organizers, the demonstration had additional sponsors that included PDX Trans Pride and Planned Parenthood. This broadened the demonstration's issue focus to include gender identity and expression as well as women's reproductive rights. After criticism from the NAACP for a lack of diversity, the demonstration looked to address racial issues for women of color too. It was a broad coalition movement that kicked off a tumultuous midterm election cycle that would be filled with liberal protests in Portland.

On many occasions, differing ideological protests clashed in the streets. Marches that took place on Eighty-Second Avenue, a major artery in Portland, pitted conservative protesters arguing for free speech on one side of the road against an angry group of liberal protesters on the other side. Months later, competing ideological protests saw the right-wing Patriot Prayer group face off with anti-fascists, leading to violence and a riot.

Liberal protests, however, clearly dominated the political arena. Demonstrators descended on the Portland airport to protest an executive order that barred the entry of millions of people from seven Muslim-majority nations including Iran, Iraq, Libya, Somalia, Syria, Sudan, and Yemen. Chants rang out at the airport, "No ban, no wall, America is for us all." One protester, Kat Stevens, from the activist group Portland Resistance, sat down with the state newspaper the *Oregonian* to reflect on the influence of the many protests, particularly immigration protests against the Muslin ban:

> And we have a community that is coming together on a weekly basis to make these protests happen. . . . The airport ban was one example where people rose up not just in Portland, but all across the US. And came together and said: "This is not okay. This is not alright. The Muslim ban is unconstitutional. We can't let that happen." And shortly thereafter it was struck down in court. These are separate occurrences. These are separate things, but I don't think it would have been easy for that to be taken down if it weren't for thousands, hundreds of thousands of people coming together and saying this is not okay. And every time we do that, we send a message and people are listening. (quoted in Kavanaugh 2018)

To offer some perspective on the spiked levels of activism in Portland and Phoenix, the average number of liberal protests for most zip code areas across the country was approximately eight events over the two years leading up to the 2018 elections. The protests that took place in Portland and Phoenix (according to zip code) overshadowed this amount. Portland (zip code 97229) residents witnessed 126 liberal protests in their area alone. Phoenix (zip code 85044) experienced 138 liberal protests. Behind the usual suspects of cities with high levels of protest, Phoenix and Portland ranked fifth and sixth, respectively, for having the largest number of liberal protests in their corresponding zip codes for those years.

One Oregon newspaper genuinely asked if there was any reason for engaging in this activity. An unexpected, and likely unintentional, answer is it led to more money for a specific party.

THE CAMPAIGN MONEY COMING OUT OF PHOENIX AND PORTLAND

Phoenix and Portland are not the home of the überwealthy, but residents in these cities can largely be classified as belonging to the middle class. While the average median household income for the entire nation as reported by the US Census in 2017 was roughly $57,652, Portland residents earned a little more with $61,532 as their median. Residents in Phoenix made slightly less than the US average with a median household income of $52,080.

The average campaign contributions to Democratic candidates do not track nicely with voters' capacity to give based on income. Actually, Phoenix and Portland are significant outliers. Allow me to establish a base understanding of giving nationally. In any random zip code across the country, the average amount of money residents gave to all political candidates combined was $24,287 for the two-year election cycle. This amount does not include contributions to national parties or political organizations; it applies solely to donations made directly to political candidates. Yet this amount does include both Republican and Democratic candidates. If we narrow our focus to only consider Democratic candidates, the average contribution coming from within a single zip code drops to $14,806. Democratic candidates did indeed receive more contributions on average than Republicans. Still, this amount pales in comparison to Phoenix's and Portland's contributions.

In Phoenix's zip code, the contribution to Democratic candidates was $36,862, more than twice the amount of the national average. The large contribution to Democratic candidates is surprising given that Phoenix's median income was less than the national average, indicating that residents in this Phoenix zip code had fewer financial resources to give. Nevertheless, they donated significantly more to liberal politicians' campaigns than other Americans. The

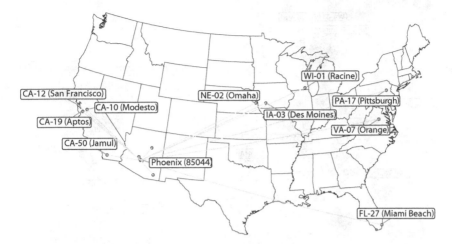

FIGURE 4.1. Democratic Contributions from Phoenix, Arizona (85044)

contributions in Portland's zip code were even greater than in Phoenix. Portland residents living in this zip code donated an impressive $60,432 to Democratic candidates. Even though the income for residents in Portland was slightly higher than the average for the nation, it is difficult to expect donations to Democratic candidates to be four times greater than the national average.

What is more interesting about campaign contributions coming from Phoenix and Portland was not how much they gave but instead where they gave. The beneficiaries of campaign contributions were not just the politicians who were running in races close by these protest-dense areas. A significant portion of donations from Phoenix and Portland poured out of the city and even out of the state. Figure 4.1 depicts the congressional races that received campaign contributions going to Democratic candidates from zip code 85044 in Phoenix. Only out-of-state contributions are labeled. Residents in Arizona saw the races of other Democrats as vital to the general party success to such a degree that they supported their efforts with dollars. Campaign contributions went to Cindy Axne, a Democratic challenger, to help her in a competitive race in Iowa's Third Congressional District; Axne went on to unseat the incumbent, David Young (R). These contributions helped Donna Shalala (D) increase her resources in Florida's Twenty-Seventh Congressional District

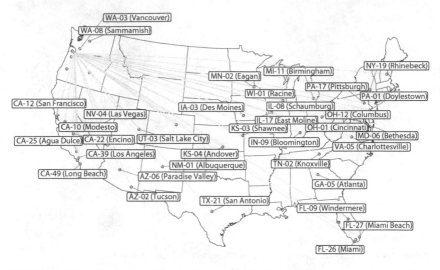

FIGURE 4.2. Democratic Contributions from Portland, Oregon (97229)

and thus defeat Maria Salazar (R). Contributions likewise went to very contentious races that helped Democrats compete, as was the case in Virginia's Seventh Congressional District, where Abigail Spanberger narrowly won a House seat with an impressive showing against incumbent Dave Brat (R).

In figure 4.2, we can see that not only did people in Portland give more than did residents of Phoenix but their contributions also went to a larger number of races outside the state. Successful democratic candidates Haley Stevens (D) from Michigan's Eleventh Congressional District, Conor Lamb (D) from Pennsylvania's Seventeenth Congressional District, Antonio Delgado (D) from New York's Nineteenth Congressional District, and Debra Haaland (D) from New Mexico's First Congressional District, among others, received financial contributions from Portland's zip code 97229. Even in uncontested races, such as the one in Georgia's Fifth Congressional District where long-serving Democratic politician and former civil rights leader John Lewis was running unopposed, Portland dollars poured in during the election cycle.

When we look at the pattern of political donations, it becomes clear that the financial gains from protest are not limited to the specific area in which that protest occurred. Campaign contributions flow to other states. This suggests that protest in one area allows politicians in other states to benefit financially.

The money coming out of Portland and Phoenix in support of liberal politicians was significant. There was clearly something different going on—something that compelled residents in these particular areas to give more money to Democratic candidates across the nation. I believe these differences stemmed from the extent to which the populations were exposed to liberal political protests. It is difficult, however, for us to draw generalizable conclusions from only two cities in the United States. Moreover, there are a host of other factors that actually could explain why Portland and Phoenix contributed more money to the Democratic political candidates than other areas. Neighboring towns could have also increased their donations that cycle, prompting residents in Portland and Phoenix to give more; the number of wealthy voters could drive up the amount of giving, and other demographic factors such as population size and the racial minority makeup could help explain the money flowing out of these areas.

To get at the heart of how protest mobilizes giving, we should expand our assessment to include the entirety of the United States and consider alternative explanations for giving. I do just that in the next section.

National Assessment of Ideological Protests and Campaign Contributions

There are two important sources of information to examine as we expand our assessment of protest and campaign contributions beyond Portland and Phoenix: the FEC's collection of campaign spending over the 2018 midterm election cycle and a daily assessment of protest. In recent years, the federal government has pushed for more transparency in campaign donations, and made it easier for average citizens to follow the money and track campaign contributions. The FEC is the primary source of this information. Since 2009, the FEC has made this information easily accessible electronically, ensuring that it is effectively disseminated for those who care to look. The information on campaign contributions is quite extensive, and includes contributions from individuals, corporations, and political action committees. All donations of $200 or more must be reported to the FEC, and are thus present in its statistics. Yet many smaller transactions are still often filed with the FEC and appear in the public database.

The FEC also keeps track of soft and hard money. I will avoid venturing too far into the weeds, but a baseline understanding of the different types of political donations could prove helpful. Contributions are considered soft money when they are given to national political parties that go to their "nonfederal" accounts. Nonfederal accounts support the costs for voter registration, corporate support for party conventions, and get-out-the-vote drives for state candidates. Voters can give an unlimited amount of soft money to national parties and nonfederal parties' funds. These donations allow voters to strengthen and grow political parties in America, especially those that share their ideological leaning.[5] Political parties use soft money to fund many of their campaign activities, but a large portion of these funds go to state activities. National parties finance state party organizations' efforts to register voters and mobilize turnout (Ansolabehere and Snyder 2000). Soft money can also be used by parties to advocate for the passage of public policies.

Hard money refers to donations in the form of contributions made directly to candidates. The majority of campaign contributions are of this type, and there are limits on hard money contributions. The 2017–18 limits specified that individuals could not give more than $2,700 to political candidates per election and no more than $33,900 to a national party committee with the intent of supporting a candidate per calendar year.[6] Individual contributions rarely approach these limits. In the 2000 election, for example, the average

5. It should be noted that soft money had a negative connotation of being linked with corruption and money laundering that still lingers today. Parties have looked to avoid FEC regulations on contribution limits by funneling national funds into state organizations, which serve as fronts for the national parties (Ansolabehere and Snyder 2000, 606).

6. Because this is per election, an individual could give $2,700 during the primary and another $2,700 during the general election.

amount that a citizen contributed was a mere $115 (Burns et al. 2001; Ansolaehere and Snyder 2000). These small donations characterize voters' contribution habits.

The examination of hard money can be revealing for understanding voters' political intent. These dollars represent individuals' purposeful actions to help a particular political candidate who not only has a distinguishing party label but also a specific background and policy platform. Given that we can trace hard money donations to the specific politician whom donors intended to support with campaign contributions, something we cannot do with soft money donations, we will focus our attention on hard money.[7]

I move beyond broad measures of protest that are seen in the form of national newspaper articles, such as the *New York Times*, to explore the influence of political activism as captured in other forms of media. References to protest in national newspapers act as a proxy for the general sentiment in the nation that is likely reflected at the local level. Voting, which is done once a year, is quite different than contributing to a political candidate because donations can be made at any point in the election cycle. And as stated earlier, the decision to contribute to a political candidate can often be an immediate reaction to citizens' local social events. The geographic consequences of this distinction require an assessment of protest at the local level that is sufficiently timely to capture the impulsive reactions of citizens who give to campaigns. To this end, this chapter incorporates protest activity as reported in multiple informational sources, including web scrapers, social media feeds, and newspaper sources.[8] As per usual, I also classify the protest events along ideological lines into liberal and conservative activism.

7. It is important to indicate, however, that giving to national parties through soft money or political candidates through hard money both feed into strengthening ideological ties, because there are polarizing ideological differences among parties and candidates.

8. I use protest data from the Crowd Counting Consortium, which captures activism since the Trump presidency began (Pressman and Chenoweth 2019). I combine these data with my own data collection efforts of protest that was reported in newspaper outlets.

PROTEST AND THE STRONG LINK TO CAMPAIGN DONATIONS

In table 4.1, I explore the various factors that potentially influence Republican and Democratic contributions. As was previously suggested, there are several factors that determine why residents in a particular zip code might donate to political campaigns. The education levels of a community heavily influence its donations, though not in the way we might think, given that education is positively related to wealth. Ironically, less educated communities are more likely to give money to political candidates, and both parties benefit from this giving. Candidates also receive more money from more densely populated areas. Yet the varying demographics of the population can drastically influence giving. Racial and ethnic minorities, for example, are less likely to donate money to political candidates. On average, political candidates from both parties will see fewer contributions from a particular zip code as the percentage of blacks and Latinos increases in that community. Finally, if citizens reside in an area where their neighbors give to political campaigns, this increases the chances that they themselves will give too, thereby supporting an earlier finding by Gimpel, Lee, and Kaminski (2006). These motivating factors are reflected in the data presented in table 4.1, but they affect Republican and Democratic candidates unevenly. Several community characteristics impacted the amount of donations that a Republican received but had little sway on the campaign resources of Democratic candidates. Donors to Republican candidates were found to be wealthier than those giving to Democrats. Furthermore, having a Republican incumbent on the ballot drew additional money to these candidates' political campaigns—another benefit that Democratic incumbents did not enjoy.

The primary difference between parties that stands out for our purposes is the influence of ideological protest. Indeed, ideological protest had a strong and significant impact on campaign contributions overall. Nevertheless, for the 2018 midterm elections, protests primarily aided the coffers of Democratic candidates. Every liberal protest that occurred in a zip code was associated on average to a

TABLE 4.1. Factors That Influence Campaign Contributions by Party

	Campaign Contributions by Party	
	Democratic Contributions	Republican Contributions
	(1)	(2)
Neighbor contributions (Dem.)	0.836***	
	(0.008)	
Liberal protests	71.517***	
	(19.623)	
Neighbor contributions (Rep.)		0.880***
		(0.011)
Conservative protests		31.750
		(204.450)
Median income	0.046	0.030*
	(0.030)	(0.013)
Education (high school)	−13.710***	−3.513***
	(0.625)	(0.288)
Population	2.826***	0.837***
	(0.117)	(0.054)
Percent of Black residents	−81.701*	−64.395***
	(38.696)	(17.769)
Percent of Latino residents	−337.898***	−152.525***
	(40.329)	(18.489)
Incumbent politician	−471.004	1,687.339**
	(1,355.162)	(623.292)
Constant	248.059	−1,855.431*
	(1,749.840)	(798.752)
Observations	30,940	30,940
R^2	0.381	0.248
Adjusted R^2	0.381	0.248
Residual Std. Error (df = 30,931)	98,981.990	45,401.510
F Statistic (df = 8; 30,931)	2,384.427***	1,275.876***

$72 increase in the total amount of donations that residents in that zip code gave to some Democratic candidate, all other things being equal. This is not an insignificant amount, given that there are more than thirty thousand zip codes in the United States. If just one liberal protest took place in each area, that would likely lead to $2.1

TABLE 4.2. Campaign Contributions by Gender and Race

	Campaign Contributions within Democratic Party:		
	Women (1)	Latinos (2)	Blacks (3)
Neighbor contributions (Women)	0.978*** (0.006)		
Gender-related protests	−22.626 (68.309)		
Neighbor contributions (Latino)		0.976*** (0.006)	
Immigration-related protests		−5.588 (6.336)	
Neighbor contributions (Blacks)			0.862*** (0.007)
Race-related protests			25.631** (8.968)
Median income	−0.015 (0.009)	−0.005 (0.003)	0.001 (0.002)
Education (high school)	−3.927*** (0.187)	−1.004*** (0.057)	−0.682*** (0.039)
Population	0.827*** (0.035)	0.213*** (0.011)	0.141*** (0.007)
Percent of Black residents	−35.927** (11.535)	−10.690** (3.574)	−2.687 (2.429)
Percent of Latino residents	−120.263*** (12.022)	−32.325*** (3.743)	−18.928*** (2.514)
Incumbent politician	−260.021 (404.850)	6.367 (125.256)	82.576 (84.650)
Constant	1,324.042* (522.097)	356.054* (161.110)	53.543 (108.951)
Observations	30,940	30,940	30,940
R^2	0.529	0.498	0.393
Adjusted R^2	0.529	0.497	0.392
Residual Std. Error (df = 30,931)	29,560.880	9,149.004	6,183.767
F Statistic (df = 8; 30,931)	4,349.585***	3,828.383***	2,499.406***

Note: *p < 0.05; **p < 0.01; ***p < 0.001

million being provided to Democratic politicians as a direct result of political activism.

We can also explore whether or not specific types of liberal protests were more strongly related to contributions allocated to a specific subset of liberal candidates. For example, do protests on women's issues motivate nearby voters to donate more to Democratic candidates who are women? Does minority protest garner additional support for minority candidates? I look at this possibility in table 4.2, assessing contributions received by Democratic women, Latino, and African American candidates. Liberal protests on women's issues were not related to an increase in contributions to the campaigns of Democratic women candidates, nor did Democratic Latino candidates see more campaign contributions from areas that experienced proimmigration protests. African American candidates, though, did greatly benefit financially from donations originating in geographic areas that experienced race-related protests. On average, one liberal protest addressing racial inequality and discrimination in a given zip code was associated with residents in that zip code contributing an extra $25 to African American candidates running for office. This would indicate that the liberal protests in Charlottesville that pushed back against anti-Semitism and white nationalism led voters in this area to provide additional resources to black Democratic candidates across the country. The satellite liberal protests that sprung up across the nation under the saying "We Stand with Charlottesville" also helped to fund the campaigns of black democratic candidates.

This result is particularly intriguing because on average, African American communities do not contribute as much money to political campaigns as their white counterparts. The lack of contributions from this minority community is unlikely due to a willingness to engage, but rather attributable to the lack of financial resources they have at their disposal. In order to give, one needs discretionary funds—a luxury that too many black communities typically are not afforded. Still, protest activism serves as a way to offset the lack of financial resources that black candidates might be able to draw from their black constituents.

TIMING OF PROTEST GIVING

We can dig even deeper to look beyond why people give and investigate how long it takes voters to contribute after an ideological protest has happened. The timing of political protests' impact could be immediate, given that issues can be fleeting. Yet the influence can also last for months or even years after the protest event occurred. The civil rights movement, for example, impacted voters' perceptions of politics long after the 1960s and continues to shape policy today. Fortunately, we can consider both the short-term impact and lingering influence of ideological protest with an autoregressive distributed lag model.

Another aspect of timing to consider is the ordering of giving: Are protests leading to campaign contributions or are campaign contributions leading to greater protests? This problem of causality is referred to as the *endogeneity of simultaneous-equation bias*. These technical terms can be simplified to mean that it is hard to determine whether money shapes political outcomes or people give because they expect a political outcome. This "which comes first, chicken-or-egg scenario" is an inherent issue of trying to understand whether campaign contributions can shape politicians' votes.

In this research design, protest and campaign contributions tend to move in one direction: voters are likely to contribute funds when they see protests. While it is unusual to see the inverse occur, it is still possible for citizens to protest over campaign contributions. This was the case in Florida when the grocery store Publix contributed to a congressional member who supported the National Rifle Association in the midst of the March for Our Lives movement, resulting in protest.[9] This research design addresses causality by constraining the timing so that protest lags behind campaign contributions because it is difficult to imagine that protesters can predict voters will give in the future and thus engage in protest today. The empirical model, then, is motivated by the theoretical notion that protesters are the first movers and voters are responding to protest activism with their

9. This approach borrows from a research design used by Thomas Stratmann (2002) to assess the impact of campaign contributions on roll call votes.

TABLE 4.3. The Timing of Campaign Contributions

	Campaign Contributions Over Time (Days):	
	Democratic Contributions (1)	Republican Contributions (2)
Democratic contributions (Lagged 1 Day)	0.538*** (0.035)	
Liberal protests	613.419** (212.735)	
Liberal Protests (lagged 1 Day)	317.666 (213.671)	
Republican contributions (lagged 1 Day)		0.418*** (0.038)
Conservative protests		−4,803.721 (3,889.293)
Conservative protests (lagged 1 Day)		2,795.507 (3,880.261)
Constant	287,487.800*** (35,445.850)	222,649.800*** (23,283.460)
Observations	571	571
R²	0.309	0.186
Adjusted R²	0.305	0.182
Residual Std. Error (df = 567)	616,071.100	387,805.100
F Statistic (df = 3; 567)	84.576***	43.299***

Note: *p < 0.05; **p < 0.01; ***p < 0.001

donations. In table 4.3, I report the short- and long-term effects of ideological protest along with its impact on a daily basis.

Once again, the influence of ideological protest is lopsided. Although conservative protest is not found to affect the contributions that Republican candidates received, the occurrence of liberal protests, on the other hand, impacts the timing of donations to Democratic candidates. On average, one liberal protest is associated with a $613 increase in the total contributions made to Democratic candidates from all zip codes. Based on our models, the impact that liberal protests have on campaign contributions is immediate. Campaign contributions are made on the same day that the protest happens; voters see protest take place and they promptly donate. The immediate response by voters to liberal protests is an indication of the passionate knee-jerk reactions that individuals have to liberal issues that include women's rights, racial discrimination, and support for gun control. Even just a few days after a liberal protest event, giving significantly decreases.

These results also show that voters are following protest activity from *afar* and largely responding by sharing their resources with Democratic political candidates from a distance. Protests inform us of where we can expect contributions to come from as activism awakens interest in specific areas. The issues highlighted by protest then let us know which ideology will benefit from this discontent.

These findings build on other scholarly work. We know that individuals are giving to candidates and issues that they care passionately about. We also know that individuals may give throughout the electoral process. What I add to this previous understanding is that salient protest moments arouse citizens' interest to the point that they use their financial resources to advocate for issues that they find important. Hidden beneath the political noise that stems from an election cycle are the protest sparks that bring salient issues to the forefront for voters and motivate giving.

Campaign giving in response to protest does not benefit both parties equally. This finding is quite different from the work of previous scholars, which has demonstrated that party contributions across local geographic areas are roughly the same. In particular, areas that give a lot to Republicans give a substantial amount to Democrats too (Gimpel, Lee, and Kaminski 2006). Conversely, my research shows that in areas that experienced heightened protest, Democrats largely benefited from the ideological link with citizens' activism.

THE MONETARY BACKLASH OF LIBERAL PROTESTS

We saw that conservative protests are not influencing voters to give to Republican candidates in the way that liberal voters donate to Democratic candidates in response to protest activism. Nevertheless, we should not interpret the relationship between protest and Republicans' campaign contributions as nonexistent.

On the contrary, we have seen that when *liberal protests* occur in the nation, campaign contributions for Republican candidates increase as well.

It appears that liberal protest can lead to a backlash of giving that supports politicians on the other side of the ideological aisle. Interestingly, conservative protests do not have this opposing effect of benefiting Democratic political candidates. Voters at times witness liberal protests that they simply disagree with and find ways to push back on these issues. Given that these voters cannot head to the voting booth at that moment, they funnel their frustrations into the coffers of political candidates they entrust to advocate for their oppositional stance. Yet the political campaign funds raised by Republican political candidates associated with liberal protest are significantly less than the campaign contributions raised by Democratic political candidates in response to the same event.

The net effect of political protests is thus more beneficial for political candidates that share the same ideology of protesters. In other words, when liberal protest occurs, everyone makes money. Democrats just make more of it.

Conclusion: Ideological Protest as an Equalizer for Campaign Contributions

A catchy saying used to solve political criminal cases of corruption tells us to "follow the money." The understanding is that by following the money, investigators can uncover the answers they seek. Just as this is key for solving criminal cases, it is helpful for uncovering an interesting link between protest and political donations. This chapter provides further support that political protest does resonate with voters throughout the election cycle. The way in which voters reveal this influence is through their campaign contributions to political candidates. Not only are voters moved to give by protest activism, but they give along partisan lines that mirror ideological priorities. Those who give serve as monetary surrogates for protesters.

Though political protesters advocate against the union of money and politics, they are indeed (at least in part) a reason why millions of dollars flow into Washington, DC. This realization is not all bad; in fact, a deep understanding of giving demographics reveals a potential cure for a known ill that plagues political giving. The amount one donates to a political party or candidate may signal the intensities of one's beliefs, but some individuals are simply more financially capable of reacting to protests' calls for action. This response could lead to a disproportionate number of citizens having a greater say in society. The outcome is unsettling, because as political philosopher John Rawls (1971, 225) lays out, "Liberties protected by the principle of participation lose much of their value whenever those who have greater private means are permitted to use their advantages to control the course of public debate." This also suggests that protest issues that resonate with wealthier segments of the electorate will generate greater financial support for the party than other concerns.

The work presented here, however, shows that protest activism levels the playing field and elicits support from members of society with moderate means. The small donations ignited by political protest accumulate and together have a massive impact on political outcomes. This revelation leads to a new understanding of protest potentially acting as an equalizing force for the great levels of inequality that traditionally operated in campaign funding and political spending. If political donations are to be seen as an act of speech, it is encouraging to recognize that perhaps a wider segment of the American public is accessing its right to participate in this dialogue.

Finally, the geographic impact of protest is fascinating. Ideological protest has a geographic rippling effect. Demonstrations that occur within a specific area have the ability to reach out beyond a unique city and financially impact political races across the country.

Thus where a protest begins is truly not where its influence ends.

5

Voter Turnout

DOES PROTEST LEAD TO VOTER TURNOUT OR PUBLIC BACKLASH? THE CASE OF BLACK LIVES MATTER

> On the black side, you have to teach your children to be
> respectful of the police. And you've got to teach your children
> that the real danger to them, 99 out of 100 times, 9900 [*sic*]
> out of a 1,000 times, are other black kids that are going to kill
> them. That is the way they are going to die. . . . And when you
> say, "Black Lives Matter," that is inherently racist. That is anti-
> American and it's racist.
>
> **—RUDY GIULIANI, FORMER MAYOR OF NEW YORK CITY ON
> CBS'S *FACE THE NATION*, 2016**

The election of 2016 was one that truly invoked change. Control of
the Senate went to Republicans, with the GOP walking away with
52 seats and the Democrats gaining just 48. The House of Representatives witnessed an even greater divide, as 241 seats went to
Republicans while only 194 seats went to Democrats. Republicans
even won three of the four competitive gubernatorial races. Even
beyond the changes in Congress, Americans woke up to a distinctly

different political climate on the morning of November 9. They knew that their barrier-breaking, black president would be gone in just a few months' time. They acknowledged that they would not witness the first woman becoming president in January. They recognized that they would chart unprecedented territory with a nonpolitician in the executive office of the US government.

The outcome was so devastating to CNN political commentator Van Jones that tears ran from his eyes as he tried to comprehend the results on the night of the election. He contemplated how he would explain Trump's victory to his children at breakfast the next morning. He blamed the upsetting outcome on a "whitelash" against a changing country and, in part, a black president. Alongside the first black president came a heightened sense of racial awareness in American society that challenged institutional racism and discrimination in the form of numerous black protest events. In large part, minority protest, organized and sustained by the Black Lives Matter movement, led this charge. The whitelash that Jones pointed to was a white-led backlash against these progressive steps toward racial equality. Jones's comments on national television suggested that white conservative voters turned out to the polls to support their political candidate, who they believed would pushback against this progress, while white liberals either flipped their vote to Republicans or stayed home.

Could progressive protest events have played a small role in mobilizing—or demobilizing—the silent majority of voters? Had protest messages succeeded in mobilizing the people who wanted to vote against the protesters' interests? Or did protest mobilize like-minded individuals to vote, but not enough to achieve its preferred electoral outcome? For sure, protest messages succeeded in striking a chord with a larger audience. When protest events appear on our television screens or the front page of our newspaper, it is easy to assume that the only people who care about the issue are the few disgruntled individuals that we can see protesting with signs and megaphones. Yet the protesting minority on the street does reflect the opinions of a larger number of people in the silent majority that decided to avoid the marches and mass demonstrations. In fact, in order for protest to resonate and have real influence, protesters have no choice but to cling to the majoritarian nature of our democracy and impact a large number of voters.

Voters are the silent majority watching protest from the comfort of their home. There are a host of reasons why voters are not actually engaging in the protests themselves. Regardless of the reason, watching the masses fill the streets on their television screens or outside their windows leads the silent majority to form an opinion of protest events. It is possible, or even likely, that these perceptions are nurtured and deepened over an election cycle until they culminate into action at the polls. Both sides of the political aisle attempt to nudge voters to the polls so that they can channel their ideological positions into a favorable vote. And as Jones suggested, progressive change, in part captured through political protest, could be at the center of enticing voters to come out to the polls.

Protest definitely has the capacity to solicit interest and garner public attention, especially given how well protest issues track with public opinion concerns. From the perspective of activists, political protest is a form of communication that individuals can rely on to express the grievances of a community and push for change against the status quo. For some observers, this message will be embraced; it will inspire passionate support and even motivate actions. Others see the protest actions as an offense to their sensibilities that should be rooted out. This discontent can also motivate action—to work against the goals of the protesters. These two worlds of protest response coexist, and often come to the forefront when tragic and momentous events occur in our history. A prime example of this is the disparate reactions to the rise of the Black Lives Matter movement, which was a response to the unprecedented number of black deaths at the hands of police in the years leading up to the 2016 elections. The interactions of Black Lives Matter activists with the general electorate shows that the response of protest activity is not only an objective process of information dissemination but indeed an emotional one that changes individual attitudes and remains with individuals long after the activism has subsided. This chapter therefore sharpens our analytic focus and looks beyond community voting to explore the duality that is seen in voters' feelings toward protest. By charting both the support for and vitriolic pushback to protest, this chapter seeks to understand how protest can mobilize individuals to turn out on Election Day.

Protest Provides a Reason to Vote

There are some people who vote in every election. These individuals are eager to participate in a general, midterm, primary, or special election, or cast their ballot for any other reason. They believe deeply in their duty and responsibility to have their voices heard. The perpetual voter will show up to the polls regardless of the changing sociopolitical issues of the day and does not have to be mobilized to turn out. Then there are some, on the other hand, who need a little encouragement or a reason to vote. It is difficult to persuade these individuals to go vote.

If you want to get voters to turnout on Election Day, mobilization is key. Mobilization can be the difference between a successful election and an unexpected upset. The most effective way to get people out to vote is through door-to-door canvasing of neighborhoods and encouraging individuals, in person, to vote (Green, McGrath, and Aronow 2013). People frequently perceive mobilization efforts as activities that the political parties organize (Huckfeldt and Sprague 1992). In many ways, this is true; political parties link up with local entities and canvas the local electorate to get voters out to the polls. Today people can even be encouraged to vote through text messages (Malhotra et al. 2011). These impersonal messages are most often useful as a way of sending information to registered voters—a group of individuals who have already signaled their interest in voting (Dale and Strauss 2009). Political parties mobilize faithful supporters and party activists, and the efforts of activists send a message to the broader public (Huckfeldt and Sprague 1992, 84). But as Lisa Garcia Bedolla (2016) wrote in the *New York Times*, even among these faithful voters, voter turnout requires voter contact from "a trusted messenger who can convey a message that resonates with the target voter's lived experience."

Communication among citizens is important, but Bedolla's assertion that the message should resonate with voters is an essential aspect of electorate engagement and a difficult one to achieve. First of all, it's quite possible the political messages that resonate with citizens over the course of an election cycle could evolve. Canvasing doors, which may lead to at most one or two interactions with voters, does not create the passion needed for political messages to resonate. Frequently, salient political events lead to shifts in the public interest to prioritize some issues over others and invoke passion for those issues. Voters are on the lookout for relevant messages and events, constantly monitoring their community and the activity occurring in their area. It is thus not surprising that increased political or policy interest is one of the primary reasons people vote (Kelleher and Lowery 2004; Dahl 1967, Iyengar and Simon 2000; Sigelman 1982; Brady, Verba, and Schlozman 1995).

Protest is the microphone that enables salient issues to peak citizens' political interest in a topic. While ideological protest can spark broad interest in bringing about liberal or conservative change, issue-specific protests that fall within these ideological camps can capture voters' interest in a particular subject matter and force individuals to consider concerns facing America. For example, when political protest highlights racial and ethnic minority concerns, the issue of race surges on the public agenda. The American public recognizes the informative cues that stem from minority protest actions—perhaps even before national governmental institutions have an opportunity to respond (Gillion 2013).

The history of Americans' fight for racial equality is a good lens to understand the mobilizing impact of protest activism on the electorate. Major black movements in the past have been used as political vehicles to mobilize individuals out to the polls. The civil rights movement concentrated on educating and informing the black community of voting through voter education projects and voter registration drives. These efforts were organized through black institutions. African American churches, for instance, frequently conveyed political messages to motivate congregants to vote (Harris 1994; Calhoun-Brown 1996). At the heart of the black church voter mobilization efforts, however, were the activities of protest organizations; during this time, churches and the protest movement became linked with one another (Morris 1984). Although the liberal wing of the Democratic Party funded the churches' efforts, its motive was to shift the activities of the movement away from violent behavior to less contentious political activities. As a consequence, the movement increased its political efficacy in the black community and mobilized individuals to the polls (Winders 1999, 852).

Apart from the salience of the issue that protest invoked, protest succeeded in swaying the black electorate because mass demonstrations challenged the status quo. This led to cynicism among citizens, where they came to question whether or not government was doing a sufficient job. This cynicism propelled racial and ethnic minorities to engage in political activity (Shingles 1981; Guterbock and London 1983). Political protest also added to the social pressure of voting as activists made explicit public appeals to minority citizens to join the fight for racial equality by heading to the polls. This social pressure was effective because it drew on individuals' desire to be part of the solution as opposed to sitting out and receiving the public scrutiny of being part of the problem (Gerber 2016). Thus protest was a strong resource for mobilizing voter turnout.

The mobilizing force of political protest is not just limited to one ideological side. The conservative Tea Party protests in 2010 pushed for change and increased Republican voter turnout (Parker and Barreto 2013). In the midst of these conservative protests, Republican voter turnout jumped 9 percent from the previous midterm election (Cook 2014). Apart from the 1994 midterm increase, this was the largest increase in three decades. The increased turnout of conservative voters benefited Republican candidates as they saw their vote share climb nearly 12 percentage points—at a time when only 1 percent of the population was engaging in Tea Party protests (Madestam et al. 2013). For this election cycle, the silent majority clearly included voters who agreed with the Tea Party protesters.

Thus far I have largely focused my characterization of political protest as being an informative signal that is well received by the public. Especially for those individuals who share a similar ideological or demographic background, protest raises the salience of political and social events, and galvanizes individuals to action. Often voters are moved to act because they believe in the sociopolitical cause voiced by activists or sympathize with the message. Yet the public's reception of protest is not a utopian fantasy in which everyone agrees with the message voiced by activists or even approves of the manner in which they are voicing their discontent. There are two sides to the public's response to political protest: political support and political backlash.

The American public's backlash to protest can be fierce, not to mention equally as passionate as the support shown by sympathizers of the protest. While much scholarly work has centered on a protest's political support, little attention has been given to the adverse reaction it produces. The rationale for political backlash to protest activism comes in different forms and is more multifaceted than political support. Understanding the root causes of the backlash is an intriguing endeavor, but this exploration is beyond the scope of my literary focus on elections. What deserves more critical attention is whether or not disapproval of protest is as strong a force for mobilizing voter turnout as is support for protest.

Those who oppose a protest often have different goals than those who support it. At times, the backlash seen by the public is not directed toward the substantive message of the protest but rather the very act of individuals protesting. Consider, for example, the activism discussed in chapter 3 relating to the NFL protests of 2017 that began with former San Francisco 49ers' quarterback Colin Kaepernick taking a knee during the singing of the national anthem. Both the protest and its supporters were looking to speak out against the increasing number of African Americans being killed by police officers as well as challenge discrimination throughout the nation. The pushback, however, was focused on the actions of NFL players during the national anthem, labeling them as disrespectful.

President Trump and Vice President Mike Pence attacked the integrity of the demonstrators, becoming the mouthpieces of the backlash. Although the public opposition wanted the players' protest actions to stop, no one put forward solutions to address the underlying grievances of the protesters. As the NFL protests decreased, largely due to a new, NFL-issued rule preventing protest in 2018, the backlash dissipated, reinforcing that the outrage was linked to protesters' actions, not their message. Though the pushback decreased, the protesters' discontent lingered on because the issue of police brutality had become more salient and was left unaddressed. As we will see later in the chapter, it is unlikely that a backlash of this kind would mobilize the opposition to the polls, but it would likely galvanize supporters.

Public backlash is probably most pronounced when protest messages involve racial issues. There is something interesting and potentially unique about race that provides a fertile ground for the American public pushback.[1] The 1950s and early 1960s witnessed some of the largest levels of protests against minority rights. The pushback in these decades featured old-fashioned white backlash to pro–civil rights protests spurred by racism, bigotry, and white fear of sharing schools, bathrooms, and lunch counters with perceived undeserving African Americans.

Protest backlash along the lines of race continued to surface in the late 1960s as President Nixon offered stark criticism to the riots that occurred in the Northeast. We saw this pattern again during the 1990s, when politicians and reporters rebuked the Los Angeles protest riots after Rodney King was beaten by police officers. Alongside many of these racial episodes of protest backlash there was also great support for protesters stemming from the black community.

The push and pull of support for protest was on full display in the two years leading up to 2016 election. And unsurprisingly, this duality of protest revolved around racial issues. It was an era that included the ascendance of the Black Lives Matter movement in response to the highly publicized deaths of black men, women, and children. These protests were deeply connected to electoral fortunes, and provide insight into how political activism is received and acted on by voters. Because protest issues of race have so often

1. Marisa Abrajano and Zoltan Hajnal (2017) expand on how this backlash, largely seen among white Americans, can impact citizens' attitudes and behavior.

resulted in public disapproval and resentment, it is a fitting issue for us to examine in greater depth. The Black Lives Matter movement, in particular, offers an opportunity to explore the potential benefits that lead voters to come out as well as its potential to act as a stimulus for those who disagree with the message. In using the Black Lives Matter movement as a case study, I will examine empirically how the movement has affected voter turnout and just how mobilizing that force can be.

Black Lives Matter: A Reawakening of Minority Protest

Following the death of Trayvon Martin, a teenager who was shot and killed while walking in his neighborhood, and the acquittal of the shooter, George Zimmerman, a group of three women decided they had witnessed enough injustice. Their frustration as well as passion gave birth to a project centered on raising awareness about the many forms of discrimination and hardship faced by black folks on a daily basis. Their project had a calling card: #BlackLivesMatter. This hashtag provided a platform for users of Twitter, Facebook, and other social media sites to comment on social injustices, and connect their arguments to a much larger discussion of the value of black lives. The conversation about black lives occurred throughout the nation. Soon, the hashtag #BlackLivesMatter grew into a network of organizations called Black Lives Matter. Pew Research found that over a five-year window, from 2013 to 2018, the hashtag #Black-LivesMatter was used nearly thirty million times and on average, seventeen thousand tweets invoked the term each day (Anderson et al. 2018).

Something greater than just a saying, though, emerged from the computer screens that touted the popular hashtag. The hashtag gave way to actual political action on the streets in the form of protests. In the aftermath of some of the most high-profile and egregious forms of racial injustice around police-related deaths of African Americans, most famously the shooting of Michael Brown and the strangling of Eric Garner, tens of thousands of protesters marched through the streets. Videos of police shootings in the United States were rampant, and Black Lives Matter seized on the moment. People blocked traffic, occupied entrances to buildings, and disturbed normal business, all in an effort to signify that police brutality cannot be accepted or normalized. The imprint of Black Lives Matter was evident throughout these protests. Protesters wore shirts with three words stacked on one another in black and white letters that read "Black Lives Matter." Massive banners were placed in the front of protest lines that read "Black Lives Matter." Children would sit atop their parents' shoulders with posters bearing the slogan. Even when Black Lives Matter did not organize minority protests, there would be various Black Lives Matter activists sprinkled throughout the crowd with a sign or shirt to keep the slogan of the movement in the public's mind. You did not have to be a card-carrying member of Black Lives Matter to carry the mantle and hold up signs. There was no national sign-up list. As long as you believed in the message and joined the cause, you were part of the movement.

The influence of Black Lives Matter clearly touched the lives of millions. The movement prompted everyday citizens to don apparel that expressed their support. World-famous celebrities such as Oscar-winning director Spike Lee and Grammy-winning singer John Legend became invested in the message; Legend was so inspired by Black Lives Matter that he wrote a song called "Penthouse Floor" in solidarity with the movement. Professional athletes such as LeBron James, Carmelo Anthony, and Serena Williams often ended their social justice tweets with support of Black Lives Matter by including the iconic hashtag. The social phenomenon of Black Lives Matter even found its way to the 2016 Super Bowl when megastar Beyoncé delivered a controversial halftime show performance of "Formation," a song expressing the sentiments of Black Lives Matter, with dancers garbed in outfits reminiscent of the Black Panther movement of the 1960s. Media outlets such as the *Washington Post* ran headlines that conveyed the sentiment of the American public: "Beyoncé is a powerful voice for Black Lives Matter. Some people hate her for it." The cable news network CNN later ran a story titled "Beyoncé Gets Political at Super Bowl, Pays Tribute to 'Black Lives Matter.'"

Black Lives Matter, however, really gained momentum as local communities began to embrace its cause. Black Lives Matter was different than previous organizations that had tackled racial inequality in the United States, especially organizations that thrived during the era of the civil rights movement. While previous well-known organizations like the NAACP or Urban League had notable leaders such as Martin Luther King Jr., Black Lives Matter was a leaderless group, largely directed and sustained by each of its members. Members of an older generation of black leadership often clashed with Black Lives Matter, and occasionally struggled to understand its goal and purpose. Nevertheless, Black Lives Matter had garnered the support of the larger black community. And though not everybody agreed with Black Lives Matter's tactics, the black community largely appreciated that it had a protest voice screaming from the darkness of despair to bring attention to racial violence and a growing system of injustice. The Black Lives Matter movement was a major phenomenon that had a newness to it. This novel but faintly familiar movement highlighted a new direction for the black community in its fight against discrimination and push for racial equality. This expression of black empowerment was less a revisiting of civil rights movement activism and more a new frontier, here to meet the evolved form of systemic oppression that remained pervasive in the United States.

Beneath all the support there lurked a strong, latent opposition. It came under the guise of inclusion, through the lens of individuals who felt that America had moved beyond the confines of race to become a postracial society. The opposition claimed it was not *just* that black lives mattered but rather that all lives mattered. This sentiment gave birth to an All Lives Matter movement. All Lives Matter also began with a hashtag, #AllLivesMatter, that often was included in tweets responding to Black Lives Matter statements. All Lives Matter shirts were also printed up and worn in public spaces. The All Lives Matter slogan, for the most part, remained just words and did not translate into political protest. Yet it became the countermovement to oppose Black Lives Matter.

The meaning of All Lives Matter was clear on the surface: not only were African American lives threatened daily and needed to be valued but white lives were also threatened and should be valued. The term "All Lives Matter" generalized the specific problem that was uniquely occurring in the black community, police brutality and racial injustice, to argue that everyone faced these forms of prejudice. All Lives Matter claims evoked defensiveness, arguments of "reverse racism," the perceived exclusivity of minority spaces, and unfair sympathetic treatment to just one group. The backlash to Black Lives Matter became so tumultuous that the movement was deemed un-American and racist by many of its critics.

Rudy Giuliani, the former mayor of New York City, appeared on CBS's *Face the Nation* to make this very point to the American people and provide a solution for the increased police-related deaths of young African Americans:

> On the black side, you have to teach your children to be respectful of the police. And you've got to teach your children that the real danger to them, 99 out of 100 times, 9,900 out of 1,000 times, are other black kids that are going to kill them. That is the way they are going to die. . . . And when you say "Black Lives Matter," that is inherently racist. That is anti-American and it's racist.

These statements were harsh, but also inaccurate on multiple levels (not the least among them being the impossibility of 9,900 out of 1,000). Be that as it may, Mayor Giuliani was not alone in his sentiments and the backlash evolved. On July 6, 2016, more than a hundred thousand individuals signed a petition to label Black Lives Matter a terror group.

Adding to the backlash, a similar countermovement emerged in response to Black Lives Matter from the very individuals whose behavior was initially being protested: law enforcement personnel. They created a campaign of their own dubbed Blue Lives Matter. The purpose of Blue Lives Matter was to bring awareness to slain police officers and their families. Yet the name was a direct response to the Black Lives Matter movement. Ironically, the day in which Black Lives Matter received the greatest number of tweets was on July 7, 2016, when five police officers were shot dead following protest events in Dallas. Many of these tweets about Black Lives Matter were negative remarks pushing back against the hostile environment that black protests had created for law enforcement. Disdain for the Black Lives Matter movement became common among police officers. Pushback against the movement was present beyond the internet as well. One group of police officers dressed in civilian clothing, for example, refused to provide security at a sporting event that featured the Women's National Basketball Association players from the Minneapolis Lynx who wore shirts that had "Black Lives Matter" printed on the front. Black Lives Matter had clearly struck a nerve in certain parts of the United States that not only saw the movement as un-American but also destructive for our society.

Electoral Connection

By the beginning of 2016, the Black Lives Matter movement had burgeoned into more than just protests against the death of unarmed black people, police brutality, and racial profiling. The protests now sought to highlight inequality in other segments of society, including mass incarceration, unemployment, and daily discrimination. As politicians discussed these issues on the campaign trail, the Black Lives Matter movement became deeply connected to the electoral process. Alongside organizing massive marches and rallies in the street, individuals who aligned themselves with the movement directly confronted political candidates on the largest of stages and in the most public of fashions.[2]

On February 25, 2016, then presidential candidate Hillary Clinton was faced with such an encounter. Clinton was holding a rally in Charleston, South Carolina, for a small audience in a private residence. Camera crews, the security detail, and guests all huddled together to listen to Clinton discuss her vision for America. In the middle of her speech, a young black woman emerged from the side of Clinton with a sign. While some were confused about what was taking place, others immediately suspected that this was yet another protest interrupting a politician's remarks—a common

2. Black Lives Matter even created a policy platform that laid out its demands.

theme reported in the news. It soon became clear that this was indeed a youth activist holding a protest sign, which read, "We have to bring them to heel." The words on her poster seemed obscure, but they held a deep meaning and revealed a damning history. These were Clinton's words, uttered twenty years earlier during a speech in which she defended her husband's, former president Bill Clinton, infamous crime bill, titled the Violent Crime Control and Law Enforcement Act of 1994.

If I offered an accurate recount of the then first lady's speech in 1996, she did mention that the nation needed to bring "them to heel." Yet it is important to know who was the ambiguous "them" to which she was referring. The statement was made in the larger context of discussing gang violence and gang members. Clinton offered the following words:

> But we also have to have an organized effort against gangs. Just as in a previous generation we had an organized effort against the mob. We need to take these people on. They are often connected to big drug cartels; they are not just gangs of kids anymore. They are often the kinds of kids that are called superpredators—no conscience, no empathy. We can talk about why they ended up that way, but first, we have to bring them to heel.

Some interpreted the first lady's speech to be an example of coded language that suggested that all African American youths were superpredators. The president's crime bill developed a greater racial connotation after its passage because it resulted in a disproportionate number of African Americans being sent to prison under its new guidelines. This only made her words seem more insensitive. Due to the political climate during her 2016 campaign, Clinton's words from two decades prior added to her vilification.

During the confrontation with the Black Lives Matter protester, Clinton read the sign aloud, but the protester cut her short, demanding that Clinton apologize for mass incarceration. Clinton ignored the command and attempted to postpone the conversation until after her speech. She began to tell the young woman that she could speak later, but Clinton was abruptly cut off again. The protester, now unrelenting in her position, emphatically stated, "I am not a superpredator." Seconds later, a security guard awkwardly wrapped his arm around the protester and whisked her away in an effort to minimize the attention that the distraction had received.

The Black Lives Matter protest resonated with Clinton, and she showed remorse for her previous statements. It was difficult to discern whether Clinton's remorse was due to a sincere change of heart or an opportunistic moment to minimize the electoral fallout, but she made it clear to the public that she regretted her remarks. The very next day, Clinton issued an apology in the *Washington Post*, writing, "Looking back, I shouldn't have used those words, and I wouldn't use them today."

Bernie Sanders, another Democratic presidential hopeful in the 2016 election, was also confronted by Black Lives Matter while campaigning. His approach was even more inviting than Clinton's. In August 2015, Sanders held a rally in Seattle in the Hec Edmundson Pavilion at Washington University that was supposed to be the second half of a two-part event. Earlier that day, Sanders had been unable to speak at the first rally, which took place at Westlake Park, because Black Lives Matter protests occupied the space. During the Westlake Park rally, Sanders hoped that he would have an opportunity to talk about Social Security and some of his progressive platform. Shortly after his opening remarks, however, Sanders was interrupted by two Black Lives Matter members. It was the one-year anniversary of the death of Michael Brown, a young African American man who was shot by a police officer in a high-profile case. In order to bring awareness to police brutality, the protesters urged the crowd to take a four-minute and thirty-second moment of silence. This gesture symbolized the four hours and thirty minutes that Brown's body lay unattended on the pavement following his shooting. Sanders yielded the stage to the protesters, and his event organizers canceled the remaining events; the captive audience of thousands that had gathered to hear from Sanders was instead witness to a reminder of its own nation's race issues through the lens of the national conversation about police brutality. Though the actions of Black Lives Matter were confrontational, protesters who felt the party and its candidates were not addressing vital issues had found another platform, and another way to force the Democratic Party to listen.

By mid-2016, Clinton, Sanders, and the Democratic Party had firmly placed themselves in full support of the Black Lives Matter movement. During the Democratic National Convention, nine black mothers who had lost their children to police brutality or street violence took to the stage on the second day of the event. These individuals were referred to as the "Mothers of the Movement." Their speeches on that day were filled with hope. Chants of "Black Lives Matter" flooded the convention hall as they stood on stage. As the cameras panned across the audience, one could see the diversity of support that ranged from white delegates cheering to older African Americans crying. It was clear that Black Lives Matter was a rallying cry for liberals.

The actions of Democrats differed vastly from those of Republicans. Notable Republicans had already joined the slowly growing chorus of Black Lives Matter critics, who lambasted the movement's divisive approach. In 2015, Republican senator and presidential hopeful Rand Paul said on Fox News' *Hannity* that he thought that Black Lives Matter should "change their name, maybe—if they were All Lives Matter or Innocent Lives Matter . . . but commandeering the microphone and bullying people and pushing people out of the way, I think, really isn't a way to get their message across." Former Republican governor of Florida Jeb Bush went further to suggest that individuals did not need to apologize for stating "All Lives Matter." While responding to a candidate who apologized for using the slogan, Bush argued, "If he believes that white lives matter, which I hope he does, then he shouldn't apologize."

When the then presidential nominee Trump was asked about the phrase Black Lives Matter, he echoed some of the same accusations of racism that had been voiced by Giuliani. Trump told the Associated Press that "a lot of people feel that it is inherently racist. It's a very divisive term, because all lives matter. It is a very, very divisive term." Although Democratic candidates experienced awkward moments in their interaction with Black Lives Matter, they acknowledged the right of protesters to exist in their rally spaces and admitted the need for policy shifts to address the very real concerns of the group. Republican candidates would not even recognize the protest movement as legitimate.

Not only was "Black Lives Matter" a racist phrase according to many Republicans, but it was threatening to them. While sitting in her seat at the Republican National Convention, a self-described "petite" white suburban mom named Melissa Stevens, who stood at five feet tall and weighed ninety-eight pounds, was asked to leave the convention for wearing a shirt that read "Black Lives Matter." The sergeant at arms informed her that she was a security threat, and asked her either to leave or remove the shirt. Stevens tearfully went to the bathroom and turned the shirt inside out.

This poses the question, were the Republicans' fears valid? Had Black Lives Matter become a serious threat? After the 2016 election ended, the Federal Bureau of Investigation (FBI) leaked a report that suggested that the movement very well might be classified as such. The FBI Domestic Terrorism Analysis Unit identified a "black identity extremist" movement, which it said had taken hold in the United States. This black identity extremist movement was defined by the FBI as a group having extreme retaliatory perceptions of lethal violence against police officers. The report goes on to indicate that this movement likely started after Brown's death in Ferguson, Missouri, on August 9, 2014. While this definition does not accurately define the Black Lives Matter movement, it very well could be an accurate assessment of the way that the federal government *saw* the Black Lives Matter movement. It is no small coincidence that the Black Lives Matter movement grew to greater prominence after Brown's death. This report carried with it an insinuation that the FBI was targeting "black" organizations that expressed sentiments against police brutality, and Black Lives Matter was by far the most notable case of such an organization.

The perception of political protest to resolve issues of racial inequality, as seen through the response to the Black Lives Matter movement, was deeply divided—but according to political ideology rather than race. On the one hand, the Democrats incorporated the movement's message formally into their national convention, and on the other hand, the Republican Party's leadership categorized the movement as a serious security threat. The electorate was attentive to these ideological protests, and the leading politicians' words and interactions with the group had added a partisan bent to the activism. While these narratives of protest response are informative, they do little to reveal whether or not the attitudes were held, consistently, across the nation, let alone whether these attitudes toward ideological protest translate into voter turnout for either side. By examining data from the American National Election Studies (ANES), we get a more definitive answer in the next section.

America's Electoral Response to Black Lives Matter by the Numbers

For every election since 1948, the ANES has conducted an assessment of citizens' thoughts about the elections. The survey is considered the primary source for citizens' electoral opinions. In the 2016 survey, the organization asked questions specifically related to Black Lives Matter. Fortunately, this allows us to further explore the support and pushback of the American public by assessing voters' attitudes toward Black Lives Matter. One survey question asked individuals to place their feelings on a thermometer scale that spanned from zero to a hundred, where zero indicated a strong dislike toward Black Lives Matter and one hundred signified a strong approval of the Black Lives Matter movement.

The ANES data showed that support for the Black Lives Matter movement was divided along the same racial and ideological lines that were often discussed in newspaper outlets. As shown in figure 5.1, African Americans held Black Lives Matter in high regard. Their feeling thermometer was over seventy on average. Although the strong support for Black Lives Matter did not vary much by age, there was more support among young individuals. Interestingly, the support for the Black Lives Matter movement among African Americans was

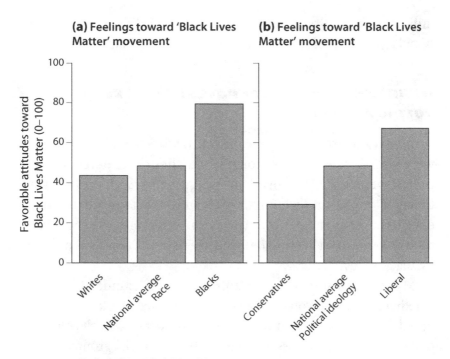

(a) Feelings toward 'Black Lives Matter' movement

(b) Feelings toward 'Black Lives Matter' movement

FIGURE 5.1. Feelings about Black Lives Matter

also greater in those states that experienced large levels of protest activity, such as Pennsylvania, Minnesota, and New York.

Support for Black Lives Matter was not constrained to African Americans. Much support was also seen under the larger liberal umbrella and found among liberal voters regardless of race. As we saw in chapter 2, this is because the underlying ideological priorities of the groups are aligned. The Black Lives Matter movement expressed concerns of inequity and justice that matched the broader issues that the Democratic Party had championed. Liberal white voters were supportive. Liberal Latinos were supportive. Liberal Asian Americans were supportive. Indeed, even though this was a primarily black issue, liberals in general joined the cause with their support.

Whites and conservatives were among the most ardent critics of Black Lives Matter—reflecting the backlash often depicted in the media. The feeling thermometer for these two groups was low, indicating high disapproval. Again, the ANES data matched the popular portrayal of Americans' attitudes toward Black Lives Matter.

WERE FEELINGS ABOUT PROTEST RELATED TO VOTING ACTIVITY?

Although the attitudes toward Black Lives Matter on both sides were strong, it is still questionable whether these perceptions of protest were related to individuals' voting behavior. If protests were to impact mobilization efforts, we should expect the greatest influence to occur in the African American community—a segment of society that is most likely to be sympathetic to the concerns put forth by Black Lives Matter.

My research shows that in 2016, protest was indeed linked to whether individuals voted. In table 5.1, I take a deep look at what influenced individuals who did vote in the 2016 elections. Each column in table 5.1 represents an assessment of different racial groups and the factors that related to their voter turnout. The first column lists factors that impact the nation as a whole, and from there, I separate out the voting activities of the different racial groups. If we consider the entire nation, irrespective of race, the traditional factors that have consistently explained voting behavior also emerge as an explanation for national voter turnout in 2016. For example, well-educated individuals turned out to vote in greater numbers than less educated ones. Wealthier citizens were more likely to head to the polls than poorer citizens; individuals' socioeconomic status was and has always been a driving force for political behavior. Arguably one of the strongest factors related to the turnout, however, was age. Older individuals were significantly more inclined to vote on Election Day in 2016. Each of these electoral outcomes mirror the traditional narrative of voter turnout.

When broken down by race, these traditional characteristics are also evident. In 2016, the individual characteristics and societal attributes that shaped white voter turnout were not much different from national turnout. We again see the heavy influence of socioeconomic status, with wealthier and more educated whites turning out to vote in greater proportion. Older whites were also more likely to

TABLE 5.1. Factors That Influence Voter Turnout

	Dependent Variable: Voted in 2016 Elections				
	Racial Differences			Ideology	
	Nation	Whites	Blacks	Conservatives	Liberals
Black Lives Matter sentiment	0.001 (0.002)	−0.001 (0.002)	0.020*** (0.007)	−0.003 (0.004)	0.014*** (0.005)
Age	0.031*** (0.003)	0.034*** (0.004)	0.048*** (0.012)	0.036*** (0.007)	0.009 (0.008)
Income	0.048*** (0.008)	0.048*** (0.009)	0.073*** (0.027)	0.047*** (0.015)	0.035** (0.017)
Female	0.130 (0.116)	0.076 (0.132)	−0.054 (0.381)	0.253 (0.236)	0.139 (0.260)
Education	0.131*** (0.027)	0.130*** (0.032)	0.050 (0.090)	0.055 (0.055)	0.140** (0.059)
Trust government	−0.115* (0.064)	−0.179** (0.077)	0.326* (0.173)	−0.057 (0.137)	−0.078 (0.151)
Tea Party sentiment	−0.003 (0.002)	−0.003 (0.003)	−0.018** (0.008)	0.016*** (0.005)	−0.023*** (0.005)
Mobilization efforts	0.038 (0.117)	0.240* (0.136)	−0.122 (0.361)	−0.346 (0.233)	0.129 (0.261)
Constant	−1.498*** (0.423)	−1.436*** (0.485)	−3.080** (1.389)	−1.511* (0.831)	−0.537 (0.946)
Observations	2,823	2,317	317	961	764
Log likelihood	−1,046.378	−808.205	−113.536	−275.212	−221.083
Akaike Inf. Crit.	2,110.757	1,634.411	245.072	568.425	460.166

Notes: Statistical significance is denoted as follows: significant at *p <.05; **p <.01; ***p <.001. The dependent variable is whether or not a respondent voted in the 2016 elections. Thus, a logistic model is used. The independent variable of interest is captured by the sentiment that individuals have to the Black Lives Matter moment, which is a thermometer scale that ranges from 0 (unfavorable) to 100 (very favorable).

cast their ballot. The one noticeable difference that emerges when we separate the subgroup of white Americans from the nation is the influence of mobilization efforts. White Americans were significantly more likely to cast a ballot on Election Day if they were personally contacted and asked to register or turnout to vote.

Although these traditional factors played a role in why white voters turned out to vote, what was clearly absent from consideration was their perception of protest activity by the Black Lives Matter movement. Yes, whites on average were strongly opposed to the Black Lives Matter movement, but not enough to allow these negative attitudes to trump traditional perspectives. This stands in stark contrast to the motivations of African Americans and their favorable attitudes toward Black Lives Matter. African Americans embraced the protest activity of Black Lives Matter, and this was strongly associated with increased turnout. More simply put, African Americans who expressed strong sentiment for Black Lives Matter had a higher probability of voting in the 2016 elections. This relationship remains durable even when other traditional explanations are considered.

The results in table 5.1 allow for a more specific, substantive example of the influence that protest has on black voter turnout. Consider this: if we compared a black voter who expressed weak support of Black Lives Matter, let's assume a thermometer score of five, to someone with a strong thermometer score, let's assume eighty, the probability of voting would be 30 percentage points higher for the individual who had greater support for the Black Lives Matter movement. The black voters' positive perception of Black Lives Matters not only was associated with voter turnout but the influence was substantial as well.

The story of protest influence on voter turnout also fits within the theoretical framework I introduced earlier on ideological mobilization. Similar to African Americans as a whole, liberal voters had positive perceptions about the Black Lives Matter movement. And like African Americans, these positive attitudes toward the movement were linked to an increased likelihood that they voted in the 2016 elections. This suggests that there were indeed ties that bound the specific concerns of the black community to overall liberal interests. Table 5.1 goes on to juxtapose the factors that influence liberal voter turnout with the factors that influence the conservative counterpart. And similar to white voters in general, even though conservatives harbored negative attitudes toward the Black Lives Matter movement, these negative attitudes were unrelated to whether they voted in the 2016 elections.[3]

3. We see a similar pattern when considering Tea Party sentiment. As shown in table 5.1, conservatives who felt positively about the Tea Party movement were

There is much to draw from this detailed overview of the individual motivations of people who voted in the 2016 elections. At the heart of these data, though, we see that protest mattered, and it mattered to those who were most affected by the grievances voiced in protest activities and those who shared a similar ideological leaning. Protest activity was in fact a mobilizing force—but only in one direction. Black Lives Matter protest activity did not produce the backlash vote that was so feared by liberal media outlets in the lead up to the elections. In short, liberals were in part motivated by the protest while conservatives' voting decisions were made irrespective of Black Lives Matter.

The individual-level assessment of motivations has been helpful, but alongside many of its benefits there are several limitations that should give us pause on whether the relationship between protest and voter mobilization has adequately been explored. There are two issues in particular that should be of concern. First, individuals are known to lie about their voting activity after an election. Individual-level surveys of voting activity often report voter turnout that is 10 to 20 percentage points higher than the actual vote counts provided by official state returns. To some extent, I understand why individuals might be dishonest about their voting activity. The 2016 elections were contentious, and the outcomes were extremely shocking. Few would want to admit that they did not partake in such a monumental and consequential political event. A second, less problematic concern is that we do not know the exact location of voters. It very well could have been the case that voters who lived closer to the epicenter of Black Lives Matter protest events were more likely to turn out on election day.

————

more likely to vote. Yet unlike the pushback toward Black Lives Matter, liberals' negative impression of the Tea Party was associated with an increased probability of voting. Hence in the case of the Tea Party, we find that both the positive support and negative backlash for the protest movement were likely mobilizing forces that motivated individuals to make it to the polls. The Tea Party is slightly different from the Black Lives Matter movement, however, because of the different periods that these movements occurred. Tea Party protests were rampant during the 2010 midterm election cycle, but the movement did not replicate this level of activism in 2016. Thus liberals and black voters may associate the Tea Party with conservative ideology as opposed to the physical protest actions.

In an ideal world, we would overcome these problems by acquiring the actual voter returns for each state, preferably broken down by congressional district. Then we would want to take a look at the actual location of every Black Lives Matter protest event. Finally, we could see from an aggregate perspective which communities were being mobilized to turn out based on the efforts of Black Lives Matter. I do just that in the next section.

Protest and Black Voter Turnout

It is difficult to gauge the voter turnout of African Americans. There is no standardized process of record keeping across the United States. For example, some states separate voter turnout data by school district, some may only track this information for particular elections, and others discard these data altogether. Similarly, even in states that track these trends, some simply do not keep information on voters' racial background. Fortunately, a resource referred to as L2 maintains a national voter database file with over 185 million registered voters. The database contains information sorted by congressional district, and has information on voters' party, gender, race, and age.[4] Using data from L2, we see some patterns of voting behavior emerge among subgroups of American voters.

Voter turnout in the United States in 2016 differed drastically from the general election four years prior. It was what many referred to as a "change election," considering that a Democrat had served as president for eight years. The Democratic presidential candidate, Clinton, had broad support from the political party, yet many were unenthusiastic about her candidacy. This was reflected in Democratic turnout, which was down across the various congressional districts, but it was particularly low in the Southeast. Figure 5.2 shows the percentage change in turnout moving from the 2012 to 2016 elections, with darker regions indicating decreased turnout. Oklahoma's

---

4. When the individual characteristics of a voter are not provided by the state or left unknown, other known identifying information is used to estimate individual traits.

FIGURE 5.2. Change in Black Voter Turnout, 2012 to 2016

Second Congressional District had an especially tremendous drop in Democratic turnout, as did Georgia's Second Congressional District, West Virginia's Third Congressional District, and North Carolina's First Congressional District. On average, Democratic turnout was down 3 percent. This could be due to the lack of urgency felt among Democratic voters in these areas; a lack of enthusiasm for Clinton may have compounded a complacent attitude that the unproven Trump had little chance of becoming president of the United States.

African American voters followed the trend of declining turnout across the country, but major decline was again identified in the Southeast, including in areas that the census indicated as having a high concentration of black residents. The decline in turnout among African Americans was not surprising and almost expected. In 2012, Obama, the first African American president, was running for reelection. The black community was eager to get him reelected, and this electrified the black voter base. Obama was not on the ballot in 2016. And though many African Americans had a deep connection with Bill Clinton when he ran for office, with Pulitzer Prize–winning author Toni Morrison referring to him as the first black president, Hillary Clinton proved to be a different candidate, and 2016 proved to be a different time, beset with criticism over her approach to black incarceration. The fact that black voter turnout declined generally between 2012 and 2016 should make it easier for us to discern the positive impact of minority political protests.

In the midst of declining black voter turnout and a lack of incentives that traditionally mobilize turnout, strong social pressure to bring about political change was on the rise in the two years leading up to the 2016 elections. This pressure was led by minority protests; many of these surges in political protest were linked to the police-related deaths of unarmed black men. For example, the death of Freddie Gray, a young African American male in Baltimore who died for inexplicable reasons a week after being in police custody, led to several protests erupting on the streets of that city. This event gripped the nation, and led to the deployment of the Maryland National Guard and a state of emergency being called. Hundreds were arrested in their effort to raise awareness of this injustice.

Only months after this event, a dashcam video surfaced that showed the death of Laquan McDonald, a seventeen-year-old black man who died as a result of a police shooting a year earlier. The officers who initially reported on the incident stated that McDonald was acting irrationally and had brandished a knife as he came toward them. In contrast, the dashcam video showed McDonald walking away from police officers before he was shot an astonishing sixteen times. The residents of Chicago as well as the nation were once again horrified by the unprovoked violence carried out by police officers. This particular case added insult to injury because it involved several corrupt cops, in addition to the officers present at the shooting, who attempted to cover up the incident. Protest erupted in the city of Chicago over this event, which continued to ignite protest activity long after the initial video of the teen's death surfaced. Some of these protests engaged directly in the political sphere to challenge Mayor Rahm Emanuel's and State Attorney Anita Alvarez's bids for reelection.

As the 2016 elections inched closer, the Black Lives Matter movement was given yet another reason to protest. This time it came from

Minneapolis, Minnesota. On July 6, 2016, Philando Castile, a black man, was shot dead in the driver seat of a car by a police officer as his girlfriend, Diamond Reynolds, watched in horror from the passenger seat. Reynold's four-year-old daughter cried from her car seat in the back as Castile was killed. This incident struck a chord with many Americans because Reynolds livestreamed her misery on Facebook in the aftermath of the shooting. Millions witnessed her raw grief. Again protest spiked. Protests were organized by multiple groups including the NAACP, Black Lives Matter, and even the Minneapolis Federation of Teachers.

The senseless deaths of black men continued. Less than two months before the election, protests erupted once again when Keith Lamont Scott was shot dead by police officers in Charlottesville, Virginia. The demonstrators blocked Interstate 85 as they walked down the streets with signs that read "Black Lives Matter." Protests escalated into violence with only weeks left before the 2016 elections.

As discussed previously, the geographic proximity of Americans to these deaths and the protests that followed increased the salience of the issue of police brutality. Some of the victims' names may be completely foreign to the average American now, a few years after the events. Or maybe the names sound familiar to some, but they struggle to explain why. If you live in the city of Minneapolis, however, references to Philando Castile are likely to be commonplace. Similarly, in 2016, when someone mentioned Laquan McDonald around citizens residing in the windy city of Chicago, strong feelings emerged. The close proximity that various residents had to the protest events sensationalized this experience.

The areas that experienced greater numbers of police-related deaths also had the highest concentration of minority protest. This frequency resulted in the issue holding saliency for voters over weeks and months after the initial protest. Cities such as Chicago, Baltimore, and Minneapolis are shaded in figure 5.3. There were also minority protests that occurred in other major metropolitan areas such as Philadelphia, Los Angeles, and New York City in response to as well as support of the initial protests.

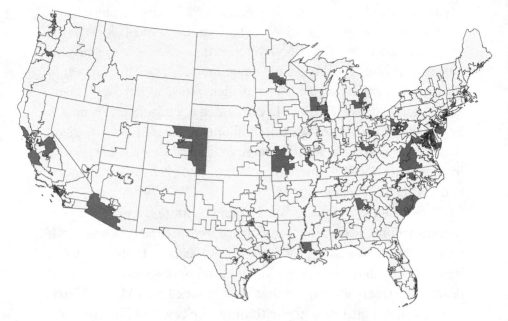

FIGURE 5.3. Areas with High Incidents of Black Lives Matter Protests (Dark Grey)

This fervent protest activity and increase in social justice work in the two years leading up to the 2016 general election harked many individuals back to the days of the civil rights movement. Many aspects of the two time periods are similar, but the characteristics of contemporary minority protests do not nicely overlap with the minority activism of yesteryear. Contrary to popular belief, protests from 2015 to 2016 were significantly less violent than protest from 1960 to 1995, as we can see from figure 5.4. There were fewer deaths that occurred, fewer reports of property damage, and fewer reports of injuries. Contemporary racial protests are also now larger and have greater organizational support then they did in the past.

The most surprising difference, especially given the impetus for many of the protests in 2015 and 2016, is that recent protests have significantly fewer events where at least one person was arrested. From 1960 to 1995, more than half the protest events involved an arrest. Today that percentage has dropped to only 7 percent of protest events.

Still, just as the 1960s' civil rights protests were instrumental in shaping voter turnout, recent protests have been successful in this

Characteristics	1960–95	2015–2016
Death occurs	0.02	0.01
Reports of property damage	0.10	0.03
Reports of injury	0.10	0.08
Lasting longer than a day	0.11	0.08
Larger than a hundred people	0.15	0.22
Reports of violence	0.17	0.11
Police are present initially	0.36	0.34
Political organization	0.043	0.54
An arrest is made	0.053	0.07

FIGURE 5.4. Comparing the Civil Rights Movement to the Black Lives Matter Movement

way as well. Though the minority protests today have slightly different characteristics than activism in the past, racial and ethnic minority protests still have the sustaining power to mobilize individuals to vote. The majority of this mobilization effort centered around protest events that were related to the Black Lives Matter movement.

The influence of the Black Lives Matter movement was most noticeable in the black community. Even though turnout was down on average for African Americans across all congressional districts, black turnout actually rose in those areas that experienced large numbers of Black Lives Matter events. If there were only a few Black Lives Matter protest events prior to the 2016 election in a community, the protest activity had little effect on mobilizing blacks to turnout. Once there were more than eight local protest events organized by Black Lives Matter, though, we start to see the impact of protest activism.

Take, for example, Minnesota's Fifth Congressional District in Minneapolis. The thirteen Black Lives Matter protest events that occurred in the congressional district of Minneapolis, many of which were sparked by Castile's death, are associated with a 2.56 percent increase in voter turnout. When we move to another part of the nation we see a similar effect. The eight Black Lives Matter protest events that took place in Pennsylvania's Second Congressional District, nestled in the heart of a large black population in the city of Philadelphia, resulted in an associated 1.57 percent rise in black voter turnout.

In the face of a "change election," declining political interest and poor national turnout among liberals and African Americans, black communities came out to vote when they were galvanized by protest actions.

Conclusion

The results of this chapter afford a deeper understanding of the impact that protest can have on the electorate. Clearly the silent majority does not respond uniformly to protest actions. Indeed, the response to protest is segmented across the electorate, with varying levels of emotional and behavioral reactions. Not only are the attitudes of the silent majority very diverse, but the ways that individuals decide to act on those attitudes are disparate. Voting turnout reflects the different responses that the public has to protest.

When protesters engage in activism, they are speaking to the masses and the American public broadly. These appeals do not go unheard; rather, they are picked up by certain segments of society. Those who are most affected by the grievances being voiced in a protest are the ones who are most likely to be attuned to the message of protest. For sure, the efficacy can be substantial for racial and ethnic minorities, as we saw with the Black Lives Movement's ability to motivate communities to the polls with sustained protest activity.

There is also a second order of influence, when the message of protesters resonates beyond those unique individuals who share in the protesters' grievances to impact voters with similar ideological leanings. White liberals who felt sympathetic to the cause of antidis-crimination work also supported the Black Lives Matter movement. Some of these remained in the silent majority—silently supporting the protest instead of opposing it—but others joined the cause.

Finally, the backlash experienced by protesters is real. Some individuals in society detest not only the message of protesters but also the very act of protesting. While these feelings of discontent might fester in the minds of opponents, the attitudes are sometimes insufficient to mobilize voting activity. The Black Lives Matter movement endured fierce, sustained pushback, and yet the net benefit of its protest activity was a positive mobilization effort for the black community and only verbal criticism devoid of action by opponents.

The pushback that any protest experiences should be expected: because protests can be seen as being ideological, there will be alliances that overlap with the United States' two-party system as well as an opposition that arises from either liberals or conservatives. This pushback, however, should not be misconstrued as an indication that protest is ineffective or counterproductive. To the contrary, protest mobilizes its ideological base to turn out on Election Day. In doing so, it takes the necessary step of linking the protest activism of a few to the voting actions of many. This is how protest matters in our democracy.

6

Election Results

A PROTEST POLITICAL CLIMATE THAT SHAPES ELECTORAL OPPORTUNITIES AND CANDIDATES' FORTUNES

> If people don't vote, everything stays the same. You can protest until the sky turns yellow or the moon turns blue, and it's not going to change anything if you don't vote.
>
> **—DOLORES HUERTA**

Voting is one of the most cherished forms of political action in a democracy. The voting process allows average citizens to play a fundamental role in reshaping their government. The history of citizens' voting preferences is a record of the political evolution of society. At any given election, voting outcomes reflect what our society wants and demands at that moment. It is the will of the people condensed down into the selection of a candidate. It is thus at this moment that the silent majority finally gets it say.

Bound within this democratic expression is the groundswell of political activism that occurs over an election cycle. This leads me to finally pose the most anticipated question of the book: Do protests influence voting outcomes? In previous chapters, we explored the contemporary impact of ideological protest on recent elections, largely within the last few years. This may have inadvertently given the impression that the impact of political protests on the electorate is a recent phenomenon. Yet dating back to the 1930s and 1940s, political activism affected elections. Protest activism during these years associated with the Townsend movement led to the election of members to Congress who were favorable to Social Security (Amenta, Carruthers, and Zylan 1992). During the height of the civil rights movement, the 1964 congressional election resulted in a new wave of liberal Democrats in the South who were less conservative than their predecessors, establishing a "generational replacement" that some argue led to shifts in voting alignments (Fiorina 1974). Are these cases of citizen activism leading to dramatic electoral changes isolated incidents, or is this a more general phenomenon?

In this chapter, I present this rich history of protest movements and their effect on the electoral decisions of the voting public. As we will see, ideological protests influence citizens all way to the ballot box. Protests also impact the early stages of the electoral process by enticing individuals to run for office, thereby changing the pool of candidates from which voters can select. This chapter brings a bounty of evidence to bear on this subject matter by drawing on more than three decades of ideological protest data and election returns from 1960 through 1995. The true revealing jewel of protest's influence, however, can be seen through the story of Abner Mikva's successful bid for office in 1968. We will explore this notable moment in history.

Electoral Decisions

OK, imagine standing in a voting booth. You see a candidate's name on the ballot and immediately reflect upon the last couple of years leading up to this decisive moment. As though you are holding a calculator, you begin to sum all the positive things that the candidate has done; let's assume each of the candidate's positive accomplishments gets one point. You think back on the negative things you dislike about a candidate's time in office and assign these shortcomings a negative point. Finally, you subtract the candidate's negative points from the positive points. If the total tally is positive, you vote for the candidate. If not, you vote for the opponent. There—you have done your civic duty of casting a vote.

This seems too simple for such a complex decision. Yet this is precisely how Stanley Kelley (1983) theorizes that voters reach decisions about political candidates when they are in the voting booth, without the handheld calculator, of course. Kelley's theory on voting decisions is surprisingly accurate for predicting how voters actually cast their ballot. The basis of his argument is sound: individuals reflect on what has transpired over the course of an election year before they decide on a candidate.

An abundance of research finds political events leave an impression on voters. These impressions are not always immediately acted on. Instead, they are stored away in memory, adding to the overall impressions that voters have about candidates (Lodge, McGraw, and Stroh 1989). As such, even though political incidents may occur months before an election, voters will still consider these salient events as they relate to each politician and support a candidate accordingly (Lodge, McGraw, and Stroh 1989).

One point of evaluation for voters are candidates' previous accomplishments, which voters use to make judgments on how politicians will perform in the future (Besley 2006). What do voters consider about an incumbent politician when they look back over the election cycle? Apart from a politician's good looks, a measure that is in fact used to evaluate candidates, voters recall favorable policies that they liked (Todorov et al. 2005). Scholars argue that some policy accomplishments, such as an improved gross domestic product or low unemployment, track well with how citizens vote (Kramer 1971; Fair 1978). In order for these elements to be persuasive, however, citizens must be aware of them—and studies show that this is not always the case (Page and Shapiro 1992).

What voters are sure to weigh heavily during the election season is how their personal life has been impacted by politics. Consequently, Andrew Healy and Neil Malhotra (2013) posit that voters ask themselves the same question that Reagan posed to the American people during his 1980 debate with Jimmy Carter: "Are you better off than you were four years ago?" (To Carter's chagrin, the answer that the electorate gave was "no" as it voted Reagan into office.) Although voters pay attention to how governmental actions will affect them, this consciousness does not always revolve around monetary benefits, as Reagan eluded to in 1980. Voters also weigh political events that divide the public along ideological lines and evaluate politicians on their response to nonpolitical events such as national disasters (Healy and Malhotra 2009).

As the electorate becomes more partisan, it considers recent current events and how candidates respond through an increasingly partisan as well as ideological lens. When ideological protests occur maybe two to three blocks from where we live, or around the corner from the grocery store where we shop, this sense of familiarity adds to the salience of the event. These monumental and transformative events are not lost on individuals. On the contrary, voters remain cognizant of them when they engage in the electoral process. Protest becomes an evaluative tool for voters as they make decisions about how to vote.

Protest as an Evaluation of Candidates' Records

When things go well in a given district, the local incumbent politician benefits and claims credit. Politicians relish in strong local economies with growing businesses, sound education systems, and low crime rates as their reputations flourish. They rely on the progress of the district as political currency for their reelection bid. If voters see their lives improving, they are inclined to credit those in charge for the positive change. When there are problems in a district, however, politicians also receive the blame.

Voters struggle at times to decipher whether a politician's previous actions contributed positively to the community's prosperity, or how. Although governing politicians often tout specific policies or laws they claim responsibility for, it can be difficult to map proposed plans—or new laws—to their effects on daily life. This is where protest becomes a barometer of political success to evaluate candidates' records. Unfortunately, activism is an unwelcomed sight for governing politicians. Put bluntly, protest signifies that there clearly is a problem.

Citizens differ on what they deem to be the many problems facing American government. Yet there is a rank ordering of which problems are more important than others on the public's agenda. When protests occur in the nation, the issue voiced in that protest rises on the public's agenda to become a greater problem that the government needs to fix (Baumgartner and Mahoney 2005; Gillion 2013). This indicates that the American public does indeed see protest issues as problems, and specifically as problems that governmental officials have a responsibility to resolve.

Politicians who represent the area in which protests occurred have no choice but to reckon with these concerns. Local-level protest forces local politicians to shoulder the blame, even if they are not the source of the problem. Adding to that pressure, though, is that local political officials are also looked upon as the extension of federal government. When people have a grievance with the federal government, local representatives are tapped as closest to the people. Thus national issues that plague society as a whole, and very well could be outside the control of congressional members, are evaluated through a local-level electorate. Constituents are discontented and want to believe that their representative is doing everything in their power to alleviate their concerns. If voters believe that a politician is not doing enough, they will hold them accountable at the polls. The blame is not always fair, but neither is the credit always deserved.

When voters witness protests in their neighborhoods, they naturally seek explanations. They want to know more about the issue being debated in the streets, what potential solutions there are, and what, if anything, representatives have done to address the problem. If they disagree with the protesters, they'll want to understand how their representatives will stand strong against the pressure of the activists. Voters carry this context and understanding with them to the ballot box. If Kelley's theory of voter decision is correct, and individuals do tally the pros and cons of electing a given politician, protest is likely to hurt the score of a lot of incumbents. This is especially the case for those who have a different ideological position than activists. The ideological bond between protests and voters allows the electorate to give politicians a negative evaluation if they failed to address an important problem.

Still, one or two protests are unlikely to sway voters' opinions.[1] These isolated incidents of activism do not spell doom for a politician. However, as political protests begin to mount in a district, they serve as a constant reminder of an unresolved issue. Hence the overflow of activism from one protest event to multiple connected events, offering repeated reminders for the public, hurts the reputation of those in office. Politicians, though, can attempt to curb the impact of protest by supporting the issues that activists highlight and showing that they are working to address the grievances. Protest aimed at existing policies or elected officials naturally spurs individuals on both sides of the aisle to dig into their ideological stance. For example, a conservative protest provides reasons for Republicans to discount their Democrat-led government's work while also mobilizing Democrats in the community to further support that government.

Because voters view protests as resulting from a problem, one might question whether there is ever a case in which politicians can salvage their electoral fortunes in the face of sustained protest activity. Or does the very presence of protests spell inescapable doom for a politician?

Protest does not necessarily mean that a politician will be punished; this is where the ideological link comes into play. The perceived ideological leaning of protest often benefits the party that has issue ownership of the activists' message. Nevertheless, the electoral consequences of protest are limited by the number of sympathetic voters who share this ideology. Republican politicians are at low risk of being hurt by hundreds of liberal protests *if* all their constituents

---

1. Though one-day massive protests, such as the 1995 Million Man March or 2017 Women's March, can have reverberating effects long after their occurrence.

are Republicans. Similarly, conservative activists face an uphill battle of influencing election results if they protest in a district with a Democrat-dominant electorate that is represented by a Democratic elected official. Ideological protest requires a coalition of voters with shared goals in order to create change at the ballot box. This need not amount to a majority of the individuals in the community, but there must be some mix of ideology among constituents for ideological protest to exhibit sway. The more diverse a district is, the more likely it is that the ideology of a protest will hold because it has the ability to engage one side. The reality is that if no local voters are involved with or sympathetic to local protest, the ideological bond is not there to shape electoral outcomes.

Voters use protest not only as an evaluative metric to consider how best to cast their ballot but also as an assessment on whether this might be an opportune time to run for office. Again, these decisions are made along ideological lines, as Democratic politicians are, for instance, seen as better equipped to remedy problems raised by liberal protest. Deciding to run for office based on protest activity, however, will undoubtedly ignite political conflict both between and within parties.

Candidates Using Protest as Insight to Gauge "Blood in the Water"

Because protest is an indication of an incumbent's job performance, it also serves as a metric to signal the vulnerability of the political candidate. In times of political unrest and frequent protest, potential political opponents may lie in wait, hoping for the right moment to run for office. Protest exposes incumbent politicians to attack, but it does not always lessen their chances of reelection. Even if potential candidates are willing and motivated to enter a political race, they must choose their moment wisely because they have the difficult challenge of unseating an incumbent. This is a formidable task given that more than 80 percent of incumbents are reelected.

At times, challengers can be deterred from running by an incumbent's fund-raising efforts (Epstein and Zemsky 1995). Successful fund-raising campaigns allow incumbents to inform voters of their previous activity through mailings and education material (Cover 1977; Cover and Brumberg 1982) as well as media outlets that are not available to challenging candidates who do not have the same access to a financial support system (Mann and Wolfinger 1980). The disproportionate flow of information from sitting politicians allows incumbents to shape their performance record in the best light. Still, protest and popular disapproval of the status quo factor into the potential challengers' considerations of political and social conditions as they assess whether they will run against an incumbent. Protest activity can also provide competing information that highlights grievances experienced during a politician's tenure.

When voters believe that incumbents have failed to deliver on promises or implement constituents' preferred policies, they can use that information to punish incumbents during their bids for reelection (Austen-Smith and Banks 1989; Ferejohn 1986). Here protest activity can act as a double-edged sword, benefiting incumbents when protesters' concerns are ideologically aligned with theirs (and the politician has demonstrated efforts to address the concern) and hindering them when they are not.

Political protest, similarly, can alert politicians of a changing tide or issue that is rising in importance. Legislators are forward-looking, concerned about future issues that could potentially endanger their seats (Arnold 1990). Thus they consider "potential preferences" that citizens may value in the future (Sulkin 2005). When legislators are inattentive to protest behavior, it provides fertile ground for challenger candidates to underscore the sitting politician's failure to address constituent concerns (Sulkin 2005).[2] The inactivity of a sitting politician also provides a political opportunity for challenging candidates who are more closely aligned with protest activists to garner grassroots support—an invaluable political currency for swaying the electorate. Hence politicians who ignore concerns voiced in

2. Tracy Sulkin (2005, 22) makes the point that "challengers may even be able to create the perception of weakness on issues simply by highlighting them in their campaigns."

district-level protest become vulnerable to political scrutiny. Protest can expose these weaknesses, making experienced challengers more likely to enter the race because they believe there is a higher chance of them winning the election (Banks and Kiewiet 1989; Jacobson 1990).

Incumbents may also face challenges to their seat from another member of their own party when protests occur in their district. At times, politicians from the same political party as voters may stray away from the preferences of their constituents. After all, constituents' preferences are constantly evolving with the political issues of the day. Politicians attempt to track these changes by following the local newspapers, checking local public opinion polls, surveying their constituents' reactions to political events, and simply talking to their constituents—tactics that political scientist Richard Fenno (2002) refers to as "soaking and poking." Politicians do, however, misstep. They get distracted with other goals and become out of touch with the same voters that placed them in office.

These troubling signs of a disconnect between a sitting politician and their constituents increase the chances that a seasoned politician decides to challenge an incumbent for a congressional seat. Like a shark sensing blood in the water, prospective candidates watch for protest levels that expose a vulnerability for incumbent politicians; it is a vulnerability that beckons potential challengers to strike and enter the electoral race. There are countless tales of ideological protest shaping political candidates' fortunes, but a favorite of mine is the story of Abner Mikva, from Chicago.

Abner Mikva and the Protests That Got Him into Office

Who is Abner Mikva? He is the original "nobody nobody sent" kid, and his story is one that Illinois politicians often tell. The story goes that a young, twenty-two-year-old Mikva, still in law school, became inspired in 1948 to help out with the Democratic Party. He was compelled to engage after reading about Adlai Stevenson and Paul Douglas, two Democratic candidates for the Illinois gubernatorial and Senate races in 1948, respectively. Mikva went into the nearby Eighth Ward Democratic Organization to offer his support. He interrupted individuals in the cigar smoke–filled room by simply asking how he could help. No one immediately responded. There was actually dead silence until an older fella who served as a ward committeeman paused for a moment from smoking his cigar and asked, "Who sent ya, kid?" Mikva responded, "Nobody sent me." The committeeman barked back at Mikva, "We don't want nobody nobody sent." This was the committeeman's way of saying that Mikva could get lost. Mikva did not go into politics that day.

Instead, Mikva finished law school and then clerked for Supreme Court Justice Sherman Minton—a great honor. Unsure what to do after clerking, Mikva turned back to politics, edged on a little by Victor DeGrazia, one of the leaders of the Independent Voters of Illinois, a liberal, antiestablishment political group based out of Chicago's Seventh Ward. DeGrazia encouraged Mikva, saying that he would be a good candidate to run for state legislator and would receive the support of the Seventh Ward.

At first Mikva was hesitant. Yet he felt that he had the type of background that could get him into office. After all, he had a law degree from the prestigious University of Chicago Law School. He had an esteemed clerkship. And he had a military background, having served in the US Army Air Corps—service to his country that voters always count as a positive. Mikva was also a persuasive speaker. He credited the practice he got as a teenager selling shoes at Nisley's, a women's shoe store. Mikva said he attempted to sell the premium shoes because you received "a bigger commission, if you sold them, maybe a dollar or even two dollars" (Horwitt 2018). So he had the gift for gab.

Mikva entered the state legislature race and won in 1956. This was his first political experience, but he went on to serve in the state senate for more than a decade. During this time, Mikva sponsored policies on fair employment practices and fair housing. However, he had his sights set on climbing the political ladder. He decided to run for the House of Representatives in 1966. Running for a federal office would prove to be more difficult than running for state office.

In 1966, Mikva ran against Barratt O'Hara, an eighty-four-year-old Democrat who enjoyed broad party support. In particular, O'Hara

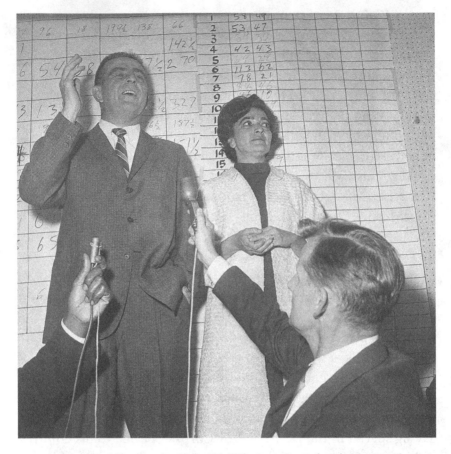

FIGURE 6.1. Abner Mikva, Standing Next to His Wife, Conceding Defeat after the 1966 Elections. Photographer: Paul Cannon (Associated Press)

had the backing of Mayor Richard J. Daley, who represented the strong and formidable Democratic machine. Still, Mikva figured he could exploit O'Hara's age by providing voters with a more youthful alternative. But with no major alliances and no experience running for federal office, Mikva was easily defeated. Mikva could have ended his political career at that moment. Instead, he decided to run for office in the very next election, in 1968.

Something was different in 1968. Nothing much had changed with Mikva. He was only two years older with roughly the same political experience. His opponent also remained relatively unchanged, a now eighty-six-year-old O'Hara. The ageism tactic that failed two years ago did not seem like a viable strategy now. And Chicago still remained a stronghold for the political Democratic machine, led by Mayor Daley. Mikva needed some help, and he got it in the form of political protest.

By 1966, Martin Luther King Jr. had taken a strong interest in Chicago. King had joined Jessie Jackson and the Southern Christian Leadership Conference's efforts to end racial discrimination in housing under a campaign called the Chicago Freedom Movement. The group looked to expand the success of the civil rights moment from the South to the North. Consequently, the movement turned its eye to Chicago, a northern city that was steeped in a racist culture at the time. King was reported as saying that the hate he saw in Chicago was worse than the hate he experienced in Mississippi. After King was hit with a rock while marching in a predominately white neighborhood on Chicago's Westside, he lamented that "I have seen many demonstrations in the South, but I have never seen anything so hostile and so hateful as I've seen here today" (*Chicago Tribune* 1966). Given the tumultuous history of Jim Crow in the South, this was saying something.

In 1967, Mikva joined the protesters' effort to combat housing discrimination in Chicago. He was no stranger to fighting for racial equality. Just a few years earlier, Mikva participated in the monumental 1963 March on Washington where King delivered his "I Have a Dream" speech. But in order to bring the protest to Chicago, Mikva would be gambling his political aspirations of making it to Congress as he confronted segments of racism in the district and a hostile Mayor Daley. However, Mikva was fighting for what he believed to be right, and so he made this protest push part of his political campaign.

Mikva soon became closely linked with the protest movement. During the campaign for fair housing, Edwin "Bill" Berry, the executive director of the Chicago Urban League, called on Mikva to attend a city hall meeting hosted by Mayor Daley. The conference gathered various black civil right leaders to address the housing problem. Although Mikva was neither a civil rights leader nor black, Berry saw Mikva as an advocate for the movement. Mikva would prove Berry right as he took up the call and campaigned for fair housing over the election cycle. Eventually, Mikva established a reputation as the fair housing advocate supporting black people in Chicago—a reputation that would stick with him throughout his political career.

Alongside the civil rights protests, Mikva championed the massive movement against the Vietnam War. He was a fierce critic of the war in Vietnam and supported the cause of the thousands of antiwar protesters who came to his district to demonstrate at the 1968 Democratic National Convention. The demonstrations were widespread and flooded the streets of Chicago near Hyde Park. Mayor Daley did not appreciate these protests in his town and unleashed twelve thousand police officers, along with support from the Illinois National Guard and army soldiers from Fort Hood. The clashing of demonstrators and law enforcement deteriorated into chaos. Hundreds of protesters were injured and arrested. "That was the most awful political experience I've ever had," Mikva said. "The convention itself, the bloodshed, the violence, the anger, the breakdown of institutions—everything went wrong, including our police department" (quoted in Dold 1996).

Mikva's support for the protesters went beyond words. The evening of the Democratic National Convention, he went to bonds court to help bail out the demonstrators who had been arrested and charged with disorderly conduct or resisting arrests. These were charges that Mikva saw as frivolous. Mikva then took his involvement a step further. He argued that the attorney general, who was appointed by Mayor Daley, could not objectively prosecute a case that involved a violation of the demonstrators' civil rights. Mikva held a press conference to ask for an independent investigator. Ronald Miller (2016, 1739), Mikva's good friend who fought alongside him, called Mikva's actions "a true profile in political courage!"

The incumbent O'Hara was noticeably absent in many of these situations. To be fair, he was an older ailing politician. But he was also enjoying the political support of Daley and the Democratic machine, and it was in Daley's interest for the protests to stop. The demonstrations made him look bad as the city's mayor. As a consequence of Daley's support, O'Hara did not speak up as protest activism reshaped his district.

Mikva, on the other hand, continued playing a high-profile role in the protests against the Vietnam War and racial housing inequality in Chicago. Minority-led protests over King's death brought additional demonstrations to the area. Through it all, Mikva was on the side of the protesters. He paid a social price for this alliance as some constituents in his district loathed him even after he was elected. The criticism that hurt the most came from white steelworkers in his district. In the years prior to the elections, Mikva had served as their attorney, helping them with their last wills and testaments as well as workers' compensation cases. But they had now turned on him, even booing him during a Labor Day parade after Mikva won the 1968 election. Historian Sanford Horwitt (2018) asked Mikva, "Was it mainly your stance on civil rights or the Vietnam War?" Mikva responded, "It was probably mainly civil rights. The war was a lot of it, too. But it was civil rights that struck home" (quoted in Horwitt 2018).

From the time that Mikva lost the election in 1966 (to O'Hara) to his victory in 1968 (over O'Hara), fifty-six liberal protests occurred in his district, reflecting a substantial amount of protest activism. The electorate validated Mikva's efforts to push back against the city's political machine and his support of protest movements. The negative sentiments of some constituents in the district were overshadowed by the support of liberal voters in Illinois's Second Congressional District. The divide between these two groups was deep, especially on racial issues, which splintered the Democratic Party in Chicago. Those who remained in the party saw Mikva's actions as a step in the right direction.

On the sails of political protest, Mikva ran for office and won. This would not be the last time this occurred.

Systematically Capturing the Relationship between Protests and Elections

By pouring through years of citizen activism and electoral returns, we can systematically assess the influence of protests on elections. In order to explore this relationship, I track protest with the well-known data source Dynamics of Collection Action, which uses newspaper events to classify protests from 1960 to 1995. I also look at voting outcomes for all 435 congressional districts over time. For each district, I capture the ideological leanings of protest within the local area. To do this, I subtract liberal protests from conservative protests in a district. When the measure is positive, the local political arena is dominated by protest activities that express liberal views; when it is negative, protests that advocate a conservative perspective have the louder voice.

While district-level protest activity may influence voters' perceptions, there are other important factors that will also shape electoral outcomes. I begin by considering often-used alternative explanations as to why a winning candidate is successful in receiving a larger percent of the two-party vote share. Arguably, the most significant factor that predicts who wins an election is the incumbency status of political candidates. Incumbents enjoy a comfortable advantage over challenging candidates when heading to the polls (Gelman and King 1990; Levitt and Wolfram 1997).[3] The advantage that incumbents receive increases over a politician's tenure in office, but this advantage has also become more significant for all incumbents over time (Ansolabehere, Snyder, and Stewart 2000).[4] In adapting this understanding to my analysis, I include a control for the incumbency advantage to account for the strong impact that characteristic has on electoral outcomes.

Two other factors likely to explain electoral outcomes are the quality of a challenging candidate and the length of time that a congressional member has served. The quality of a candidate, as described in academic literature on voting, refers to whether a political candidate has previously held office. In analyzing the quality of a challenging candidate as a dependent variable, several scholars have shown that experienced candidates, who have previously served

3. Quality candidates are less likely to enter an electoral race when an incumbent is running for reelection (Banks and Kiewiet 1989; Huckshorn and Spencer 1971; Leuthold 1968).

4. The rise in television has increased the incumbents' advantage too (Prior 2006).

in office, fare better than do inexperienced ones (Huckshorn and Spencer 1971; Leuthold 1968). Thus I incorporate the quality of a candidate as a control variable when testing the impact of protest on electoral returns. As for a representative's length of service, younger congressional leaders may be less likely to maintain a strong vote share because they have not developed the name recognition, nor have they established the proven record of their senior colleagues. Hence I control for the number of years that a representative has served in office.

I also account for other demographic factors that could foreseeably impact the election. I control for congressional districts located in southern states and the population size of the congressional district. Hopefully, considering all these additions will allow us to see the impact of protest activity alongside some well-known alternative explanations.[5]

Table 6.1 shows the impact of protest on congressional members' vote share. I distinguish the two-party vote share received from Democratic and Republican candidates to examine whether or not protest has a distinct impact on the different ideological perspectives. Indeed, the social context of protest appears to motivate different segments of the electorate and produces divergent effects on the candidates' vote share. When the coefficient on our protest measure is negative (indicating that the claims voiced in protest in a district are more conservative), the Republican vote share of the two-party vote increases. The impact of protest is reversed for the Democratic vote share: when the coefficient on my protest measure is positive (indicating a more liberal position taken by activists), Democrats enjoy a larger portion of the two-party vote.

Importantly, the magnitude of these effects is quite substantial. For example, if the salience score of liberal protest in a district is 50 in an election year, these activities are associated with a 7 percent *decrease* in the Republican vote share but a 2 percent *increase* in the Democratic

5. While control variables will account for much of the variation across districts, there may remain an omitted district-level variable that could bias the results. Thus for each model, I include fixed effects for both district and year.

TABLE 6.1: Protest Influence on Candidates Vote Share

	Republican Vote Share (1960–1990)	Democratic Vote Share (1960–1990)
Previous vote share	0.52*** (0.02)	0.64*** (0.02)
Protest$_t$	−0.12* (0.06)	0.04† (0.02)
Protest$_{t-1}$	0.07 (0.06)	0.02 (0.02)
Incumbent$_t$	6.91*** (0.54)	5.43*** (0.63)
Incumbent$_{t-1}$	2.24*** (0.51)	−3.32*** (0.46)
Challenger Quality$_t$	−3.25*** (0.41)	−3.82*** (0.42)
Challenger Quality$_{t-1}$	−0.26 (0.36)	−0.23 (0.41)
Southern district	0.65 (0.52)	−0.10 (0.45)
Length of service	0.06* (0.03)	0.05* (0.02)
Population of the district	−0.09 (0.24)	−0.06 (0.16)
N	1597	1907
R^2	0.57	0.57
adj. R^2	0.55	0.56
Resid. sd	6.15	6.82

Notes: Statistical significance is denoted as follows: significant at $^†p < .10$; $^*p < .05$; $^{**}p < .01$; $^{***}p < .001$. The dependent variables are the Republican portion of the two-party vote as well as the Democratic portion of the two-party vote, respectively. The independent variable of interest, protest, is placed on a liberal-conservative scale, where negative values indicate that the majority of protests events in a district expressed a conservative perspective while positive values indicate a more liberal position.

vote share.[6] This specific fluctuation was the case for Mikva, who benefited from protest activity in 1968. During this year, forty protest events occurred in Illinois's Second Congressional District, expressing liberal concerns that ranged from civil rights to antiwar protests. The protest salience score from these events was 54, indicating a 2 percent increase in the Democratic vote share and 7 percent decrease in the Republican vote share. Representative Mikva ran on a platform that supported these liberal concerns. He not only defeated the more moderate incumbent Democrat in the primary, O'Hara, but he went on to defeat the Republican challenger, Thomas Ireland.

6. Recall in chapter 2 that we measure the salience of a protest by summing the different characteristics of that protest event (that is, the size of protest, duration, organizational support, violence, etc.).

Republican candidates also benefit from protest activity when that activity espouses conservative issues. If the salience score of conservative protest was negative 50, indicating conservative protests, Republicans would *increase* their vote share by 7 percent, while Democrats would experience a *decrease* in their vote share of 2 percent.[7] In 1974, in Cleveland, for instance, several protest events occurred that confronted drug use in local neighborhoods and petitioned the police to take a stronger stance.[8] The salience score from these conservative protest events was negative 21, providing a 3 percent increase in the Republican vote share. These protest events aided Republican representative William Stanton in his victory over the Democratic challenger Michael Coffey in the 1974 election for the Eleventh Congressional District house seat.

Notice that there is not a one-to-one trade-off between the losses and gains of the Republican Party's vote share to the Democratic vote share. Republican voters are more responsive to the salience of protest activity. Protest activity is three times more likely to impact the Republican than the Democratic vote share. This finding is surprising given that liberal protest activities substantially outnumbered conservative ones during the time period under study. Perhaps it is the case that because liberal protest activity was so much more common during this period than conservative protest, conservative activism was more surprising, and as such, was met with a greater response by voters.

These results hold up against other competing explanations. As expected, the incumbency advantage in both models is strong. The positive coefficient on the length of service shows that candidates

---

7. Given the construction of our protest salience measure, there are myriad ways in which a salience score of 50 might be obtained. For instance, a district could have 50 events, each with a salience score of 1 (if, for example, all these events each had more than a hundred participants). Or it could have a score of 50 if there were ten protest events, each with a score of 5.

8. The war on drugs has been a Republican issue since Dwight David Eisenhower's establishment of the US Interdepartmental Committee on Narcotics in 1954, followed by Nixon's message that drug abuse is "public enemy number one," and Nancy Reagan's "just say no" campaign.

who have spent more time in office receive an additional boost in the two-party vote share. The quality of the candidates also serves to explain their vote share. As suggested by previous scholarship (for example, Cox and Katz 1996; Huckshorn and Spencer 1971; Leuthold 1968), more experienced candidates fare better in my analysis. Finally, like previous researchers (for example, Gelman and King 1990), I find that demographic features of the district are not significant predictors of the vote share; neither population size nor being located in a southern state influenced our dependent variable.

These results offer support for the theory of ideological protest and reveal that activism serves to reinforce citizens' political attitudes as opposed to changing the ideological leaning of individual's beliefs. Protest is well received among voters who already share a similar ideological perspective.

PROTEST AS A SIGNAL OF VULNERABILITY

Table 6.2 presents the relationship between protests in a district and the decision for quality challenging candidate to run for office. There are several factors that discourage experienced political challengers from running for office—one of the most significant being an incumbent politician running for reelection. This deterrent effect is seen by both Democrats and Republicans, with quality Democratic candidates being more susceptible to failure when facing an incumbent candidate. In addition to the incumbency status, the length of an incumbent's service affects a challenger's chances of winning. This dampens the likelihood that we would see a quality Republican challenger emerge in an election race to run against a well-established politician. While the regression results highlight several factors that would discourage potential challengers, protest events stand out as an impetus for electoral competition.

To further illustrate the effect of political protest, we graph the predicted probabilities of a quality Democratic candidate running for office given different levels of protest activity that express liberal concerns. As one might expect, the average salience level of protest in a congressional district is relatively low, with many of the raised

TABLE 6.2: Protest Encouraging Experienced Challengers to Run

	Quality Democratic Challenger Runs	Quality Republican Challenger Runs
Challenger Quality$_{t-1}$	−0.331** (0.102)	0.358*** (0.080)
Protest$_t$	0.014* (0.006)	−0.001 (0.003)
Protest$_{t-1}$	0.009 (0.007)	−0.000 (0.003)
Previous vote share	−0.023** (0.008)	−0.033*** (0.004)
Incumbent$_t$	−1.105*** (0.156)	−0.762*** (0.120)
Incumbent$_{t-1}$	0.193 (0.147)	0.034 (0.091)
Southern district	−6.394 (6.612)	−0.072 (0.097)
Length of incumbent's service	0.002 (0.009)	−0.020*** (0.005)
Population	0.002* (0.001)	−0.001 (0.000)
N	1597	1907
AIC	1892.656	1743.855
BIC	9182.352	1965.987
log L	409.672	−831.928

Notes: The dependent variables are the quality of the challenging candidates running for office. We incorporate Jacobson's (1980, 1990) measure of candidate quality, a measure also used by Cox and Katz (1996), which is coded as 1 if a challenger has previous held office and 0 otherwise. The independent variable of interest, protest, is placed on a liberal-conservative scale, where negative values indicate that the majority of protests events in a district expressed a conservative perspective while positive values indicate a more liberal position. Regression coefficients come from a probit model. Statistical Significance is denoted as follows: significant at *p <.05; **p <.01; ***p <.001.

ticks in figure 6.2 clustering in the single digits. But as the context of protest changes, becoming larger or more contentious, or gleaning the support of liberal political organizations, quality Democratic challengers recognize an opportunity to benefit from the disgruntled sentiments expressed in a district. As figure 6.2 shows, the predicted probability curve rises sharply with the increase of liberal-leaning protest activity, moving from a low probability of a quality Democratic candidate emerging, less than 20 percent, to a relatively higher probability, almost 50 percent, holding all other variables constant at their means.

This was the case for New York's Second Congressional District in 1974. Liberal protest in favor of gay rights, feminist groups marching against gender discrimination, and black and Latino neighborhoods rallying for greater representation in government produced a

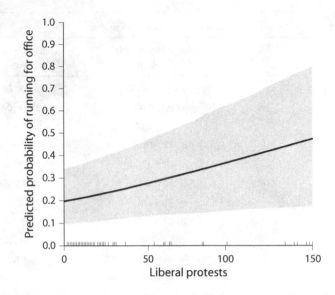

FIGURE 6.2. Probability an Experienced Democratic Challenger Runs as the Level of Protest Increases

high liberal protest salience score of 147 in the district. This significantly increased the probability of a quality Democratic challenger entering the 1974 election. Indeed, Democrat Thomas Downey, who previously served as a New York legislator for Suffolk County from 1972 to 1974, emerged to challenge the Republican incumbent, James Grover. In this particular case, Downey's bid to run for office in New York during a heightened level of liberal protest activity proved to be a shrewd decision. Downey defeated the ten-year incumbent, becoming one of the youngest members of Congress at age twenty-five.

These results are illuminating. Not only are voters informed and mobilized by protest activities, but potential candidates view protest activity as a signal that the timing is right to enter a race. That is, protest salience not only affects the public's political engagement but also provides information to would-be challengers about citizens' concerns. In turn, as quality challengers enter races, the political opportunity structure for subsequent protest may be altered. To most scholars (for example, Tarrow 2011), the political opportunity structure is more or less open to claims made by challenging groups.

And as Sarah Soule and colleagues (1999) note, protest activity can alter the political opportunity structure such that subsequent protest is more or less likely. The findings in this chapter suggest that perhaps one mechanism by which protest impacts the political opportunity structure is by encouraging quality challengers to enter electoral contests.

Interestingly, protest has not been an impetus for new Republican challengers to join the field. Here it is Democratic challengers who are more likely to recognize and act on an opportunity. But why do quality Democratic challengers respond to protest activities and Republicans do not? The history of protest in the second half of the twentieth century offers some insight. Since the majority of protests expressed liberal concerns, it is possible that Democratic challengers have become more familiar with recognizing protest as a potential cue that can mobilize the party's base.

Conclusion

Some candidates who take advantage of a contentious political environment bristling with protests are simply opportunistic. Others, however, believe that protests are a call to serve and that they are best equipped to tackle the situation. In other words, not all politicians are vultures, feeding on political protest to expose a vulnerable politician. Some see their political expertise as the necessary solution to address the political turmoil that has been voiced by protests. In this way, these individuals come across to voters as being altruistic and looking to serve the greater good. They avoid the negative stigma of seeking office purely for political ambition—a motivation that can corrupt a politician and damage their reputation. After all, as Thomas Jefferson (2004, 134) famously expressed it, "Once a man has cast a longing eye on [political office], a rottenness begins in his conduct."

Protest has long been a form of civic engagement that citizens rely on to voice their grievances. Given that there is not an institutional procedure to recognize the views of protesters, however, it is questionable whether the concerns voiced in protest activities are incorporated into the considerations of governmental institutions. Only recently have scholars of movement behavior and political participation begun to ask whether protest events can influence government. Yet the lion's share of this work has focused on the effect of protest on governmental policy, and only a few studies have looked at its effects on electoral outcomes.

This chapter provides novel insights that push our understanding forward. Protest can have dramatic effects on electoral outcomes, in two different ways. First, protest can draw voters' attention to salient issues, educate voters on a topic, and lead them to vote for candidates whose platforms and ideological positions are consistent with the grievances expressed by protest. Second, the information provided by protest events can send a signal to potential challenger candidates that the timing is right to enter a race. The empirical evidence is consistent with these arguments: protests that espouse liberal views lead Democrats to receive a greater share of the two-party vote in House elections, whereas protests that champion conservative views stimulate support for Republican candidates. Moreover, experienced (or quality) Democratic candidates are more likely to run for office when there is a higher level of liberal protest activity. Thus protest not only influences who jumps into the race but also who emerges as victorious.

This chapter suggests that citizens filter the information supplied by protest through their own ideological prisms and then use this information to inform their voting much in the same way that individuals' level of political engagement is shaped by their social context (Cho and Rudolph 2008; Eulau and Rothenberg 1986; Huckfeldt and Sprague 1995). The new perspective offered here is important because it introduces local protest activity into a discussion that has largely focused on social networks and organizational membership to understand local-level political decisions. Protest events occurring in voters' communities are sources of political information that do not go unnoticed by the local electorate.

Conclusion

A CHANGE IS GONNA COME . . .
A PROTEST CHANGE IS ALWAYS
GONNA COME

At last we have walked through the electoral process. It has been a winding road revealing voters' reactions to protest across the country and throughout history. In looking back on this journey, it is important for us to end where we began, with a consideration of the silent majority and loud minority, and for us to definitively answer the question of whether or not political protesters shape perspectives of the larger electorate.

Let's return to the White House Oval Office in 1969, with President Nixon at the Wilson Desk, draped by American flags and calling on the silent majority to support his efforts in Vietnam—the moment that fuels our curiosity about the relationship between protesters and the electorate. Even as Nixon created a wedge between demonstrators on the streets and citizens at home, protest actions contradicted the president's words and feverishly guided electoral fortunes. Party platforms were being changed, more money was being raised for those individuals who supported the protests, more political candidates were deciding to run for office, and more people were being mobilized to turn out for the upcoming election in 1970. Protest was speaking to the silent majority, and Democratic politicians would benefit at the polls from this liberal activism.

History repeated itself in 2017. Donald Trump's surprising electoral victory in 2016 sparked civic activism throughout the country. An onslaught of sustained liberal protest swept across the nation and ushered in a change in the House of Representatives that favored Democrats in the 2018 midterms, symbolizing a societal change happening in America. The silent majority that Trump touted and asked to stand with him in 2016 turned on the Republicans in 2018, voting many of them out of office—the result of a "blue wave" of protests igniting electoral engagement.

The fallacy of a silent majority standing in opposition to the loud minority protesting has been debunked. Both the Vietnam War protests in 1968 and liberal protest nearly fifty years later indicate that the silent majority is indeed swayed by the loud minority of protesters in the streets. But beyond these two elections, the previous chapters revealed the instrumental power that protest has in shaping American democracy in general. This work highlighted protest's influence at each major stage of federal elections. Political activists make their presence known early in the electoral process—sometimes the day after the previous elections. These early stages of activism offer insight into a community's concerns and grievances. Protests motivate individuals to begin or increase donations to the campaign pockets of politicians who share the ideology of the activists' message. And though protest might occur geographically in one district, activism spurs citizens to send money to out-of-state candidates in races taking place in other parts of the country.

As Election Day approaches, local protests heighten political interest within a community. They also stoke passion among voters who are more closely aligned with the activists' message, thereby mobilizing those individuals to turn out to the polls. An engaged electorate that has been energized by protest activity suggests political trouble is on the horizon for incumbent politicians who seek to minimize problems in their district. The same political protest, however, provides an electoral opportunity for seasoned challengers, encouraging them to run for office.

Finally, protests shape voting decisions. Voters use protest as an evaluative tool to assess a sitting politician's performance over the election year. This is one place where ideological protest is especially effective. The presence of more liberal-leaning protests signifies problems that Republicans are ill equipped to handle, and conservative protests present concerns that Democrats cannot credibly address. Thus by appealing to a shared underlying ideology that resonates with and signals to sympathetic segments of the electorate, citizens' activism leads their preferred candidates to receive a greater number of votes on Election Day.

Just one protest, happening in one city, on one day, can have a rippling effect on the entire electoral process. A social movement, bound with multiple protests, over multiple days, and across multiple cities, can lead to a political revolution.

The answer is clear: protests influence the electorate. Now, what does this mean for our democratic future?

The Hope in Protest, the Fear in a Polarized Ideology

Ideological protest is a political conundrum that plays to our democratic hopes and fears. On the hope side, protest is inspiring and informative. It inspires citizens to care about issues—whether this means agreement with protesters or not—and motivates individuals to participate in the political process in new ways. Protest also provides important information for citizens to consider as they communicate with one another through the public forum of deliberative democracy. The founders of America were aware of this potential power when they endowed every citizen with the right to protest. They embedded in the First Amendment of the US Constitution the right to peacefully assemble by prohibiting Congress from creating any legislation that would take away this right. To drive home the point, the Fourteenth Amendment prohibited state governments from restricting this right. The founders saw this right as a crucial mechanism for the public to express its concerns not only to the government but also to the American people more broadly. Chief Justice Hughes described the right to assembly alongside the "opportunities for the communication of thought and the discussion of public questions" (*Cox v. New Hampshire* 1941). As a consequence, protest has become a conduit of democratic appeals that shape how the majority in this nation thinks. The format of protest, fueled by citizens' passion, allows for an engagement in deliberative democracy and communicates the most salient issues to the American people.

Government entities are attuned to the democratic displays of public protest. Even more, protest serves as a second layer of checks on the system of checks and balances across the various actions of political government—applying pressure to federal governmental entities that shifts presidential rhetoric, congressional policy, and Supreme Court decisions. No institution is beyond protest's reach (Gillion 2013; 2016).

Given their wide influence, protest activities have become commonplace. They are no longer taboo or reserved for the most aggrieved members in society. For some, it is even the political tool of choice. In the 1970s, only one out of twenty people reported that they had engaged in some form of protest. By 2018, however, that number had grown to one out of ten individuals who participated in some form of political protest. American protest knows no bounds. No one is above engaging in activism. Protest activities are now being conducted by our mothers, fathers, brothers, sisters, sons, and daughters. It is the thing to do. Kate Fricke, a mother of two who we heard from in our earlier discussions of Portland, Oregon, expressed as much:

> The night after the election was the first real protest any of us had been to. I was driving my daughter to dance class and she had a friend in the car and we heard on the radio that there was a protest downtown. They were like, "Mom, can we go?" and I was like, "Absolutely." I turned the car around and we went downtown and just marched with everybody and screamed obscenities and it was pretty awesome to see the girls get so involved. They felt empowered. So that sort of became our thing. (quoted in Kavanaugh 2018).

Because protest is catching on, a greater proportion of the public is becoming politically aware and electorally involved. This means that more electoral futures will be shaped by protests. Thus the hope of protest—that individuals, and especially marginalized groups, can impact governmental outcomes and the American electorate—is becoming increasingly likely.

Some will be uneasy with the notion that a small group of demonstrators can sway the masses into a decision. The very idea invokes thoughts about the creation of a "tyranny of the minority"—a dangerous concept for a democratic system that relies on upholding majoritarian preferences. Yet the influence of protest has always been substantial. At the heart of social movements there still remains the proven formula of holding massive demonstrations in the street that persist for days, months, or even years. The activities are the same, and the influence is still potent, but the audience has changed. American society has become more attuned to politics and less informed of the political contours of the story, unable to suspend judgment for the time it takes to really listen to both sides. The influence of protest, then, possesses a catch-22 for American society. It has led individuals to see the best in those who share a similar ideology, and hear out their story as well as sympathize with their point of view. However, it has also led individuals to immediately discount the credibility of protest messages that fail to offer a similar ideological position. What the founders could not see or predict is the divisive nature in which peaceful assembly would be assessed. This is where the fear of ideological protest emerges.

In the midst of the hopeful vision of the world in which average people can shape elections and hence their government, there is a darker side of ideological protest. The actions of protest feed into the growing polarization that has torn our American civilities apart. Shouldn't we want a world in which political activism brings everyone together, not just those who have similar ideological preferences? Has the political line of "us" versus "them" shifted from being the silent majority against the loud minority to now being the Republican versus the Democrat? Does the recognition of protest's influence add to our fear of becoming a more divided

America? The answers to these questions are "yes," "no," and "yes, but let me explain."

Yes, we would all want a utopian world in which every voter could empathize with the hardship of every protester. Given individuals' differing political preferences, this simply cannot take place. But this does not move us to a situation in which protests create this new "us" versus "them" split across the political parties.

No, protesters do not establish the institutional divide of parties, but protests do work within that environment. Party leaders and organizers decide which issues they are going to embrace and champion in their platforms. These decisions create issue ownership over time, constructing a lens through which protest messages are evaluated. The political line between Republicans and Democrats certainly exists, but it is not the doing of activism.

Finally, yes, protest is likely adding to our fears of becoming a more divided America because ideological protest does reinforce and even harden positions that we have on divisive issues. But more explanation is needed here. While the political divide still remains, there is an underlying commonality that brings diverse social movements together under a shared ideological umbrella. The big divide between the two parties has to be reconciled with the coming together of the different factions that exist within the party. Protest does deepen the divide that has been caused by polarization. Within each half of this ideological divide, however, there are more individuals coming together to support separate yet related causes. Thus protest influence does not indicate that America is becoming more divided across all issues; rather, the main thing that divides us is becoming more pronounced.

Watering Down the Message or Alienating Support

In the end, protest becomes influential because it implicitly unites segments of the electorate that have different unique interests but share a common ideology. While this book has been dedicated to showing the positive aspects of these ties that bind, there indeed are some negative consequences, chief among them being the dilution of protesters' concerns by politicians once they take office. This dilution is evidenced by the broad policy agenda that politicians have a tendency to adopt once elected in order to appease the largest coalition. Ideological protest might put into office those politicians who share a similar ideological leaning with the protesters, but once these politicians are in office, they are limited in terms of what they can address within a congressional session.

When politicians attempt to pass targeted policies, they risk alienating members of the coalition. Nevertheless, some issues must be sacrificed, and because politicians are cognizant of their reelection goals, they are strategic in their policy efforts to maximize a voting coalition that will keep them in office. This often means that the interests of smaller factions within a coalition are marginalized or ignored altogether.

African Americans, for example, questioned their loyalties to the Democratic Party in 2016 amid protest actions. They felt as though the Democratic Party had taken them for granted; they were seen as belonging to the Democratic camp while having their grievances ignored for more pertinent concerns. This perspective was aided by a young generation of "woke" African Americans who believed elections were simply not solving the problems it faced in American society. Even an older generation suggested moving from contributing to elections. Eddie Glaude offered a controversial idea at the time: show up to the polls and cast a blank vote for presidential candidates. This "blank-out campaign" would send a message to the Democratic Party that more needs to be done to help out the black community. These grievances were made prominent after Democrats had achieved electoral success with Obama in 2012.

The anxiety of African Americans raises a larger concern regarding the potential effectiveness of ideological protest: it benefits one party over the other because that party is viewed as being more capable of resolving the issues that protest brings to light. The credibility of a party on the protest issue at hand is what fuels campaign giving and mobilizes voter turnout. If a segment of voters in the electorate doubt that a party can resolve their concerns, they are likely to splinter off to a more welcoming political party, or even worse, become politically inactive. The black community is just one among many factions of the Democratic Party that may come to see the party as being incapable of addressing the concerns voiced in protest.

Thus although ideological protest may be beneficial in bridging social movements across various issues, leading to electoral success, it also puts pressure on politicians to create diverse policies that appease a more diverse constituency. In order for politicians to continually garner electoral success from citizens' activism, they must be able to read the protest tea leaves and respond to the change that is coming.

Ideological Protest and Political Change

Sam Cooke was a legendary songwriter, most well-known for the song, "A Change Is Gonna Come." It is a song that causes you to rock back and forth to take in its deep, sultry sound. For those who remember his record debuting, and especially those in the minority community, the song's words would roll off the tongue. What is fascinating, though, is how this song came to be.

Cooke was traveling with his band in 1963 and happened upon a Holiday Inn in Shreveport, Louisiana. Looking to get a day's rest, he walked into the lobby and asked for a room. The Holiday Inn employees refused to allow him to stay at the hotel. Sam was shocked and angered by the encounter, but resistant to move. Writer Peter Guralnick said that when Cooke "refused to leave, he became obstreperous to the point where his wife, Barbara, said, 'Sam, we'd better get out of here. They're going to kill you.'" As an African American, Cooke was not surprised that racism existed in Louisiana. He had become all too familiar with these racial injustices as a young boy growing up in Mississippi. But he was no longer that boy. He was now a well-known songwriter who dazzled audiences and sold thousands of records. Cooke was still black, but he was a famous black man. And racism did not occur to famous black people, or so he thought. Thus Cooke responded to his wife's words by saying, as

Guralnick relayed it, "'They're not gonna kill me; I'm Sam Cooke.'" Cooke's wife brought him back to earth and replied, "'No, to them you're just another . . .' you know." Guralnick (2014) omitted the slur when describing what took place, but his audience knew what his wife meant just as well as Cooke did.

Sam Cooke was arrested and later taken to jail, along with his band members. The entire experience shook him to his core. The incident festered inside Sam's mind until he found an outlet for his frustrations in the best way he knew how: through song. Within two months, Sam wrote the famous song "A Change Is Gonna to Come." The song spoke of a hopeful future that was on the horizon in the midst of racial discrimination and inequality.

The major protest movement at the time, the civil rights movement, was drawn to the song and touted it as an anthem. The song became an instant classic among those protest activists who sought to reach the optimistic future that Cooke predicted in his lyrics. Indeed, protest activity was followed by major pieces of federal legislation that did lead to change.

Cooke's sultry song is also emblematic of ideological protest. Ideological protest signifies political change that politicians cannot afford to ignore. Much about political protest relates directly to politicians. Politicians can no longer operate as though political protest falls outside formal electoral institutions and hence is inconsequential to their political fortunes. Protest has always foreshadowed the most radical changes that occurred in American history across issues of gender, race, religion, and sexual orientation, among many others. Protest is sounding off the political alarms early in the election cycle. It is shaping spending, mobilization efforts, and political interests months before Election Day. These early signs predict future electoral outcomes.

Protests are the canaries in the coal mines that warn of future political and electoral change. Thus when protest occurs, we can expect, in the words of the songwriter Sam Cooke, that "a change is gonna come"—a change that reflects the evolving will of the people. This is democratic progress.

In the end, this progress cannot be stopped. You can either learn to walk with it or be forced to walk behind it, but it is always forward moving.

If you stop for a moment and listen closely, you can hear it. The steady pounding of demonstrators' feet. The ruffling of protest signs being hoisted up and down. The echoing chant in the distance. It is the slow beating heart of American democracy.

REFERENCES

Abrajano, Marisa, and Zoltan Hajnal. 2017. *White Backlash: Immigration, Race, and American Politics*. Princeton, NJ: Princeton University Press.

Abramowitz, Alan. 2010. *The Disappearing Center: Engaged Citizens, Polarization, and American Democracy*. New Haven, CT: Yale University Press.

Abramson, Paul R., and John H. Aldrich. 1982. "The Decline of Electoral Participation in America." *American Political Science Review* 76 (3): 502–21.

Alexander, Mark C. 2003. "Campaign Finance Reform: Central Meaning and a New Approach." *Washington and Lee Law Review* 60 (3): 767–839.

Amenta, Edwin, Bruce G. Carruthers, and Yvonne Zylan. 1992. "A Hero for the Aged? The Townsend Movement, the Political Mediation Model, and U.S. Old-Age Policy, 1934–1950." *American Journal of Sociology* 98 (2): 308–39.

Amenta, Edwin, Kathleen Dunleavy, and Mary Bernstein. 1994. "Stolen Thunder? Huey Long's 'Share Our Wealth,' Political Mediation, and the Second New Deal." *American Sociological Review* 59 (5): 678–702.

Anderson, Monica, Skye Toor, Lee Rainie, and Aaron Smith. 2018. "Activism in the Social Media Age." Pew Research Center. Accessed February 16, 2019. http://www.pewinternet.org/2018/07/11/activism-in-the-social-media-age/.

Andrews, Kenneth T. 1997. "The Impacts of Social Movements on the Political Process: The Civil Rights Movement and Black Electoral Politics in Mississippi." *American Sociological Review* 62 (5): 800–19.

Andrews, Kenneth T., Kraig Beyerlein, and Tuneka Tucker Farnum. 2016. "The Legitimacy of Protest: Explaining White Southerners' Attitudes toward the Civil Rights Movement." *Social Forces* 94 (3): 1021–44.

Ansolabehere, Stephen, and James M. Snyder Jr. 2000. "Soft Money, Hard Money, Strong Parties." *Columbia Law Review* 100 (3): 598–619.

Ansolabehere, Stephen, James M. Snyder Jr., and Charles Stewart III. 2000. "Old Voters, New Voters, and the Personal Vote: Using Redistributing to Measure the Incumbency Advantage." *American Journal of Political Science* 44 (1): 17–34.

Appy, Christian. 1993. *Working-Class War: American Combat Soldiers and Vietnam*. Chapel Hill: University of North Carolina Press.

Arnold, R. Douglas. 1990. *The Logic of Congressional Action*. New Haven, CT: Yale University Press.

Austen-Smith, David, and Jeffrey Banks. 1989. "Electoral Accountability and Incumbency." In *Models of Strategic Choice in Politics*, edited by Peter C. Ordeshook, 121–49. Ann Arbor: University of Michigan Press.

Bandy, Joe, and Jackie Smith. 2005. *Coalitions across Borders: Transnational Protest and the Neoliberal Order*. Lanham, MD: Rowman and Littlefield.

Banks, Jeffrey S., and D. Roderick Kiewiet. 1989. "Explaining Patterns of Candidate Competition in Congressional Elections." *American Journal of Political Science* 33 (4): 997–1015.

Barber, Michael J., Brandice Canes-Wrone, and Sharece Thrower. 2016. "Ideologically Sophisticated Donors: Which Candidates Do Individual Contributors Finance?" *American Journal of Political Science* 61 (2): 271–88.

Bartels, Larry M. 1996. "Uninformed Votes: Information Effects in Presidential Elections." *American Journal of Political Science* 40 (1): 194–230.

———. 2002. "Beyond the Running Tally: Partisan Bias in Political Perceptions." *Political Behavior* 24 (2): 117–50.

Baskir, Lawrence, and William Strauss. 1978. *Chance and Circumstance*. New York: Random House.

Baumgartner, Frank R., and Christine Mahoney. 2005. "Social Movements, the Rise of New Issues, and the Public Agenda." In *Routing the Opposition: Social Movements, Public Policy, and Democracy*, edited by David S. Meyer, Valerie Jenness, and Helen Ingram, 65–86. Minneapolis: University of Minnesota Press.

Baybeck, Brady, and Scott D. McClurg. 2005. "What Do They Know and How Do They Know It?" *American Politics Research* 33 (4): 492–520.

Bedolla, Lisa Garcia. 2016. "Direct Voter Contact Is Key to Boosting Turnout." *New York Times*, October 17. Accessed December 20, 2018. https://www.nytimes.com/roomfordebate/2016/10/17/how-to-energize-demoralized-voters/direct-voter-contact-is-key-to-boosting-turnout.

Bélanger, Éric, and Bonnie M. Meguid. 2008. "Issue Salience, Issue Ownership, and Issue-Based Vote Choice." *Electoral Studies* 27 (3): 477–91.

Bernhardt, Dan, Stefan Krasa, and Mattias Polborn. 2008. "Political Polarization and the Electoral Effects of Media Bias." *Journal of Public Economics* 92 (5–6): 1092–104.

Besley, Timothy. 2006. *Principled Agents?: The Political Economy of Good Government*. Oxford: Oxford University Press.

Black, Merle. 1978. "Racial Composition of Congressional Districts and Support for Federal Voting Rights in the American South." *Social Science Quarterly* 59 (3): 435–50.

Blee, Kathleen M., and Kimberly A. Creasap. 2010. "Conservative and Right-Wing Movements." *Annual Review of Sociology* 36 (1): 269–86.

Brady, Henry E., Kay Lehman Schlozman, and Sidney Verba. 1999. "Prospecting for Participants: Rational Expectations and the Recruitment of Political Activists." *American Political Science Review* 93 (1): 153–68.

Brady, Henry E., Sidney Verba, and Kay Lehman Schlozman. 1995. "Beyond SES: A Resource Model of Political Participation." *American Political Science Review* 89 (2): 271–94.

Brown, Clifford W., Jr., Lynda W. Powell, and Clyde Wilcox. 1995. *Serious Money: Fundraising and Contributing in Presidential Nomination Campaigns.* Cambridge: Cambridge University Press.

Bullock, Charles S. 1981. "Congressional Voting and the Mobilization of a Black Electorate in the South." *Journal of Politics* 43 (3): 662–82.

Burack, Cynthia. 2008. *Sin, Sex, and Democracy: Antigay Rhetoric and the Christian Right.* Albany: State University of New York Press.

Burns, Nancy, Donald R. Kinder, Steven J. Rosenstone, Virginia Sapiro, and the National Election Studies. 2001. "American National Election Study, 2000: Pre- and Post-Election Survey." Inter-university Consortium for Political and Social Research, Study 3131. Accessed July 23, 2019. http://www2.gsu.edu /~polacb/cb2000nes.pdf.

Button, James W. 2016. *Blacks and Social Change: Impact of the Civil Rights Movement in Southern Communities.* Princeton, NJ: Princeton University Press.

Calhoun-Brown, Allison. 1996. "African American Churches and Political Mobilization: The Psychological Impact of Organizational Resources." *Journal of Politics* 58 (4): 935–53.

Campbell, Angus, Philip E. Converse, Warren E. Miller, and Donald E. Stokes. 1960. *The American Voter.* Chicago: University of Chicago Press.

Cano, Ricardo, and Dustin Gardiner. 2018. "Arizona Teachers Plan Protest Wednesday over Low Pay." Azcentral.com. Accessed July 22, 2019. https://www .azcentral.com/story/news/local/arizona-education/2018/03/06/arizona -teachers-plan-protest-march-7-over-low-pay/400936002/.

Carmines, Edward G., and James A. Stimson. 1989. *Issue Evolution: Race and the Transformation of American Politics.* Princeton, NJ: Princeton University Press.

Carsey, Thomas M. 2001. *Campaign Dynamics: The Race for Governor.* Ann Arbor: University of Michigan Press.

Carsey, Thomas M., and Geoffrey C. Layman. 2006. "Changing Sides or Changing Minds? Party Identification and Policy Preferences in the American Electorate." *American Journal of Political Science* 50 (2): 464–77.

Chicago Tribune. 1966. "Dr. King Is Felled by Rock."

Cho, Wendy K. Tam, and Thomas J. Rudolph. 2008. "Emanating Political Participation: Untangling the Spatial Structure behind Participation." *British Journal of Political Science* 38 (2): 273–89.

Chong, Dennis. 1991. *Collective Action and the Civil Rights Movement.* Chicago: University of Chicago Press.

Claassen, Ryan L. 2007. "Floating Voters and Floating Activists." *Political Research Quarterly* 60 (1): 124–34.

Clement, Scott, and John C. Green. 2011. "The Tea Party and Religion." Pew Research Center, February 23. Accessed July 19, 2019. https://www.pewforum .org/2011/02/23/tea-party-and-religion/.

Conover, Pamela Johnston, and Stanley Feldman. 1981. "The Origins and Meaning of Liberal/Conservative Self-Identifications." *American Journal of Political Science* 25 (4): 617–45.

Cook, Rhodes. 2014. "CQ Voting and Elections Collection." CQpress.com. Accessed November 3, 2018. http://library.cqpress.com/elections/document .php?id=rcookltr-1527-94205-2636422&type=hitlist&num=25.

Cooke, Sam. 1964. "A Change Is Gonna Come." *Ain't That Good News*. RCA Victor Records.

Costain, Anne N., and W. Douglas Costain. 1987. "Strategy and Tactics of the Women's Movement in the United States: The Role of Political Parties." In *The Women's Movements of the United States and Western Europe: Consciousness, Political Opportunity, and Public Policy*, edited by Mary Fainsod Katzenstein and Carol McClurg Mueller, 196–213. Philadelphia: Temple University Press.

Cover, Albert D. 1977. "One Good Term Deserves Another: The Advantage of Incumbency in Congressional Elections." *American Journal of Political Science* 21 (3): 523–41.

Cover, Albert D., and Bruce S. Brumberg. 1982. "Baby Books and Ballots: The Impact of Congressional Mail on Constituent Opinion." *American Political Science Review* 76 (2): 347–59.

Cox, Gary W., and Jonathan N. Katz. 1996. "Why Did the Incumbency Advantage in U.S. House Elections Grow?" *American Journal of Political Science* 40 (2): 478–97.

Cox v. New Hampshire. 1941. 312 U.S. 569.

Dahl, Robert A. 1967. *A Preface to Democratic Theory*. Chicago: University of Chicago Press.

Dale, Allison, and Aaron Strauss. 2009. "Don't Forget to Vote: Text Message Reminders as a Mobilization Tool." *American Journal of Political Science* 53 (4): 787–804.

Damore, David F. 2004. "The Dynamics of Issue Ownership in Presidential Campaigns." *Political Research Quarterly* 57 (3): 391–97.

Davenport, Christian, Sarah A. Soule, and David A. Armstrong. 2011. "Protesting while Black?" *American Sociological Review* 76 (1): 152–78.

Dold, R. Bruce. 1996. "Dissenting Opinion." *University of Chicago Magazine* 88 (6). Accessed July 27, 2019. https://magazine.uchicago.edu/9608/9608Mikva .html.

Durham, Martin. 2000. *The Christian Right: The Far Right and the Boundaries of American Conservatism*. Manchester: Manchester University Press.

Earl, Jennifer, Andrew Martin, John D. McCarthy, and Sarah A. Soule. 2004. "The Use of Newspaper Data in the Study of Collective Action." *Annual Review of Sociology* 30 (1): 65–80.

Earl, Jennifer, Sarah A. Soule, and John D. McCarthy. 2003. "Protest under Fire? Explaining the Policing of Protest." *American Sociological Review* 68 (4): 581–606.

Eisinger, Peter K. 1973. "The Conditions of Protest Behavior in American Cities." *American Political Science Review* 67 (1): 11–28.

Epp, Derek A., John Lovett, and Frank R. Baumgartner. 2014. "Partisan Priorities and Public Budgeting." *Political Research Quarterly* 67 (4): 864–78.

Epstein, David, and Peter Zemsky. 1995. "Money Talks: Deterring Quality Challengers in Congressional Elections." *American Political Science Review* 89 (2): 295–308.

Eulau, Heinz, and Lawrence Rothenberg. 1986. "Life Space and Social Networks as Political Contexts." *Political Behavior* 8 (2): 130–57.

Fair, Ray C. 1978. "The Effect of Economic Events on Votes for President." *Review of Economics and Statistics* 60 (2): 159–73.

Fenno, Richard F., Jr. 2002. *Home Style: House Members in Their Districts*. London: Pearson.

Ferejohn, John. 1986. "Incumbent Performance and Electoral Control." *Public Choice* 50 (1–3): 5–25.

Fetner, Tina. 2008. *How the Religious Right Shaped Lesbian and Gay Activism*. Minneapolis: University of Minnesota Press.

Fiorina, Morris P. 1974. *Representatives, Roll Calls, and Constituencies*. Lanham, MD: Lexington Books.

Fowler, James H., and Cindy D. Kam. 2007. "Beyond the Self: Social Identity, Altruism, and Political Participation." *Journal of Politics* 69 (3): 813–27.

Francia, Peter L., John C. Green, Paul S. Herrnson, Lynda W. Powell, and Clyde Wilcox. 2003. *The Financiers of Congressional Elections: Investors, Ideologues, and Intimates*. New York: Columbia University Press.

Gamson, William A., and David S. Meyer. 1996. "Framing Political Opportunity." In *Comparative Perspectives on Social Movements*, edited by Doug McAdam, John D. McCarthy, and Mayer N. Zald, 275–90. Cambridge: Cambridge University Press.

Gelman, Andrew, and Gary King. 1990. "Estimating Incumbency Advantage without Bias." *American Journal of Political Science* 34:1142–64.

Gerber, Alan. 2016. "Why Get-Out-the-Vote Drives Rarely Work." *New York Times*, October 17. Accessed March 3, 2019. https://www.nytimes.com/roomfordebate/2016/10/17/how-to-energize-demoralized-voters/why-get-out-the-vote-drives-rarely-work.

Gillion, Daniel Q. 2012. "Protest and Congressional Behavior: Assessing Racial and Ethnic Minority Protests in the District." *Journal of Politics* 74 (4): 950–62.

———. 2013. *The Political Power of Protest*. Cambridge: Cambridge University Press.

———. 2016. *Governing with Words*. Cambridge: Cambridge University Press.

Gimpel, James G., Frances E. Lee, and Joshua Kaminski. 2006. "The Political Geography of Campaign Contributions in American Politics." *Journal of Politics* 68 (3): 626–39.

Gimpel, James G., Frances E. Lee, and Shanna Pearson-Merkowitz. 2008. "The Check Is in the Mail: Interdistrict Funding Flows in Congressional Elections." *American Journal of Political Science* 52 (2): 373–94.

Giuliani, Rudy. 2016. "Interview with John Dickerson on Face the Nation." CBS News, July 10.

Grant, J. Tobin, and Thomas J. Rudolph. 2002. "To Give or Not to Give: Modeling Individuals' Contribution Decisions." *Political Behavior* 24 (1): 31–54.

Green, Donald Philip, Mary C. McGrath, and Peter M. Aronow. 2013. "Field Experiments and the Study of Voter Turnout." *Journal of Elections, Public Opinion and Parties* 23 (1): 27–48.

Green, Donald Philip, and Bradley Palmquist. 1990. "Of Artifacts and Partisan Instability." *American Journal of Political Science* 34 (3): 872–902.

———. 1994. "How Stable Is Party Identification?" *Political Behavior* 16 (4): 437–66.

Green, Donald Philip, Bradley Palmquist, and Eric Schickler. 1998. "Macropartisanship: A Replication and Critique." *American Political Science Review* 92 (4): 883–99.

———. 2002. *Partisan Hearts and Minds: Political Parties and the Social Identities of Voters.* New Haven, CT: Yale University Press.

Großer, Jens, and Arthur Schram. 2006. "Neighborhood Information Exchange and Voter Participation: An Experimental Study." *American Political Science Review* 100 (2): 235–48.

Guralnick, Peter. 2014. "Interview with NPR Staff: Sam Cooke and the Song That 'Almost Scared Him.'" National Public Radio, February 1.

Guterbock, Thomas M., and Bruce London. 1983. "Race, Political Orientation, and Participation: An Empirical Test of Four Competing Theories." *American Sociological Review* 48 (4): 439–53.

Hamer, Fannie Lou. 1964. "Testimony before the Credentials Committee, Democratic National Convention." Speech at the Democratic National Convention, Atlantic City, NJ, August.

Harris, Fredrick C. 1994. "Something Within: Religion as a Mobilizer of African-American Political Activism." *Journal of Politics* 56 (1): 42–68.

Healy, Andrew, and Neil Malhotra. 2009. "Myopic Voters and Natural Disaster Policy." *American Political Science Review* 103 (3) 387–406.

———. 2013. "Retrospective Voting Reconsidered." *Annual Review of Political Science* 16 (1): 285–306.

Heller, Nathan. 2017. "Is There Any Point to Protesting?" *New Yorker*, August 14. Accessed July 17, 2019. https://www.newyorker.com/magazine/2017/08/21/is-there-any-point-to-protesting.

Hellman, Deborah. 2013. "Money Talks but It Isn't Speech." *Minnesota Law Review* 95 (3): 953–1002.

Horwitt, Sanford D. 2018. *Conversations with Abner Mikva: Final Reflections on Chicago Politics, Democracy's Future, and a Life of Public Service.* Lawrence: University Press of Kansas.

Huckfeldt, R. Robert, and John D. Sprague. 1987. "Networks in Context: The Social Flow of Political Information." *American Political Science Review* 81 (4): 1197–216.

———. 1992. "Political Parties and Electoral Mobilization: Political Structure, Social Structure, and the Party Canvass." *American Political Science Review* 86 (1): 70–86.

———. 1995. *Citizens, Politics, and Social Communication: Information and Influence in an Election Campaign.* Cambridge: Cambridge University Press.

Huckshorn, Robert Jack, and Robert C. Clark Spencer. 1971. *The Politics of Defeat: Campaigning for Congress*. Amherst: University of Massachusetts Press.

Huddy, Leonie. 2015. "Group Identity and Political Cohesion." In *Emerging Trends in the Social and Behavioral Sciences*, edited by Robert A. Scott, Marlis Buchmann, and Stephen M. Kosslyn, 1–14. Hoboken, NJ: John Wiley and Sons.

Huddy, Leonie, Stanley Feldman, and Christopher Weber. 2007. "The Political Consequences of Perceived Threat and Felt Insecurity." *Annals of the American Academy of Political and Social Science* 614 (1): 131–53.

Iyengar, Shanto, and Adam F. Simon. 2000. "New Perspectives and Evidence on Political Communication and Campaign Effects." *Annual Review of Psychology* 51 (1): 149–69.

Jacobs, Anton K. 2006. "The New Right, Fundamentalism, and Nationalism in Postmodern America: A Marriage of Heat and Passion." *Social Compass* 53 (3): 357–66.

Jacobson, Gary C. 1990. "The Effects of Campaign Spending in House Elections: New Evidence for Old Arguments." *American Journal of Political Science* 34 (2): 334–62.

Jefferson, Thomas. 2004. "From Thomas Jefferson to Tench Coxe, May 21, 1799." In *The Papers of Thomas Jefferson, Volume 31: 1 February 1799 to 31 May 1800*, edited by Barbara B. Oberg, 132–34. Princeton, NJ: Princeton University Press.

Johnson, Stephen D. 2000. "Who Supports the Promise Keepers?" *Sociology of Religion* 61 (1): 93–104.

Johnston, Richard. 2006. "Party Identification: Unmoved Mover or Sum of Preferences?" *Annual Review Political Science* 9 (1): 329–51.

Johnston, Richard, Michael G. Hagen, and Kathleen Hall Jamieson. 2004. *The 2000 Presidential Election and the Foundations of Party Politics*. Cambridge: Cambridge University Press.

Jones, Jeffrey M. 2018. "Americans' Identification as Independents Back Up in 2017." Gallup, January 8. Accessed July 20, 2019, https://news.gallup.com/poll/225056/americans-identification-independents-back-2017.aspx.

Kavanaugh, Shane Dixon. 2018. "Portland's Year of Protests: Did They Matter?" *Oregonian*. Accessed January 20, 2019. https://www.oregonlive.com/portland/2017/11/portlands_year_in_protests.html.

Kelleher, Christine, and David Lowery. 2004. "Political Participation and Metropolitan Institutional Contexts." *Urban Affairs Review* 39 (6): 720–57.

Kelley, Stanley. 1983. *Interpreting Elections*. Princeton, NJ: Princeton University Press.

Kenny, Christopher B. 1992. "Political Participation and Effects from the Social Environment." *American Journal of Political Science* 36 (1): 259–67.

King, Brayden G., Keith G. Bentele, and Sarah A. Soule. 2007. "Protest and Policymaking: Explaining Fluctuation in Congressional Attention to Rights Issues, 1960–1986." *Social Forces* 86 (1): 137–63.

King, Brayden G., and Sarah A. Soule. 2007. "Social Movements as Extra-Institutional Entrepreneurs: The Effect of Protests on Stock Price Returns." *Administrative Science Quarterly* 52 (3): 413–42.

King, Martin Luther, Jr. 1967. "Beyond Vietnam: A Time to Break the Silence." Speech at Riverside Church, New York, April.

———. 1994. *Letter from the Birmingham Jail*. San Francisco: HarperCollins.

Klandermans, P. G. 2014. "Identity Politics and Politicized Identities: Identity Processes and the Dynamics of Protest." *Political Psychology* 35 (1): 1–22.

Kramer, Gerald H. 1971. "Short-Term Fluctuations in U.S. Voting Behavior, 1896–1964." *American Political Science Review* 65 (1): 131–43.

Kuhner, Timothy K. 2014. *Capitalism v. Democracy: Money in Politics and the Free Market Constitution*. Stanford, CA: Stanford University Press.

Lee, Taeku. 2002. *Mobilizing Public Opinion: Black Insurgency and Racial Attitudes in the Civil Rights Era*. Chicago: University of Chicago Press.

Leuthold, David A. 1968. *Electioneering in a Democracy: Campaigns for Congress*. Hoboken, NJ: John Wiley and Sons.

Levendusky, Matthew. 2009. *The Partisan Sort: How Liberals Became Democrats and Conservatives Became Republicans*. Chicago: University of Chicago Press.

Levitt, Steven D., and Catherine D. Wolfram. 1997. "Decomposing the Sources of Incumbency Advantage in the U.S. House." *Legislative Studies Quarterly* 22 (1): 45–60.

Lilla, Mark. 2017. *The Once and Future Liberal: After Identity Politics*. New York: HarperCollins.

Lodge, Milton, Kathleen M. McGraw, and Patrick Stroh. 1989. "An Impression-Driven Model of Candidate Evaluation." *American Political Science Review* 83 (2): 399–419.

Lohmann, Susanne. 1994. "Information Aggregation through Costly Political Action." *American Economic Review* 84 (3): 518–30.

Luders, Joseph E. 2010. *The Civil Rights Movement and the Logic of Social Change*. New York: Cambridge University Press.

Macdonald, Stuart Elaine, and George Rabinowitz. 1987. "The Dynamics of Structural Realignment." *American Political Science Review* 81 (3): 775–96.

MacKuen, Michael B., Robert S. Erikson, and James A. Stimson. 1989. "Macropartisanship." *American Political Science Review* 83 (4): 1125–42.

MacKuen, Michael B., Robert S. Erikson, James A. Stimson, Paul R. Abramson, and Charles W. Ostrom Jr. 1992. "Question Wording and Macropartisanship." *American Political Science Review* 86 (2): 475–86.

Madestam, Andreas, Daniel Shoag, Stan Veuger, and David Yanagizawa-Drott. 2013. "Do Political Protests Matter? Evidence from the Tea Party Movement." *Quarterly Journal of Economics* 128 (4): 1633–85.

Malbin, Michael. 2012. "48% of President Obama's 2011 Money Came from Small Donors—Better than Doubling 2007. Romney's Small Donors: 9%." Campaign Finance Institute, February 8. Accessed July 21, 2019. http://cfinst.org/Press /PReleases/12-02-08/Small_Donors_in_2011_Obama_s_Were_Big_Romney _s_Not.aspx.

Malhotra, Neil, Melissa R. Michelson, Todd Rogers, and Ali Adam Valenzuela. 2011. "Text Messages as Mobilization Tools: The Conditional Effect of Habitual Voting and Election Salience." *American Politics Research* 39 (4): 664–81.

Malka, Ariel, and Yphtach Lelkes. 2010. "More Than Ideology: Conservative-Liberal Identity and Receptivity to Political Cues." *Social Justice Research* 23 (2): 156–88.

Mann, Thomas E., and Raymond E. Wolfinger. 1980. "Candidates and Parties in Congressional Elections." *American Political Science Review* 74 (3): 617–32.

Mason, Lilliana. 2015. "'I Disrespectfully Agree': The Differential Effects of Partisan Sorting on Social and Issue Polarization." *American Journal of Political Science* 59 (1): 128–45.

———. 2016. "A Cross-Cutting Calm." *Public Opinion Quarterly* 80 (S1): 351–77.

Mason, Lilliana, and Julie Wronski. 2018. "One Tribe to Bind Them All: How Our Social Group Attachments Strengthen Partisanship." *Political Psychology* 39 (S1): 257–77.

McAdam, Doug. 1982. *Political Process and the Development of Black Insurgency, 1930–1970*. Chicago: University of Chicago Press.

McAdam, Doug, and David A. Snow. 1997. *Social Movements: Readings on Their Emergence, Mobilization, and Dynamics*. Oxford: Oxford University Press.

McAdam, Doug, and David A. Snow. 2010. *Readings on Social Movements: Origins, Dynamics and Outcomes*. Oxford: Oxford University Press.

McAdam, Doug, and Yang Su. 2002. "The War at Home: Antiwar Protests and Congressional Voting, 1965 to 1973." *American Sociological Review* 67 (5): 696–721.

McAdam, Doug, and Sidney Tarrow. 2010. "Ballots and Barricades: On the Reciprocal Relationship between Elections and Social Movements." *Perspectives on Politics* 8 (2): 529–42.

McCarthy, John D., and Mayer N. Zald. 2001. "The Enduring Vitality of the Resource Mobilization Theory of Social Movements." In *Handbook of Sociological Theory*, edited by Jonathan Turner, 533–65. Boston: Springer.

McDonnell, Mary-Hunter, and Timothy Werner. 2016. "Blacklisted Businesses." *Administrative Science Quarterly* 61 (4): 584–620.

McGirr, Lisa. 2015. *Suburban Warriors: The Origins of the New American Right*. Princeton, NJ: Princeton University Press.

McKelvey, Richard D., and Peter C. Ordeshook. 1986. "Sequential Elections with Limited Information." *Social Choice and Welfare* 3 (3): 199–211.

McPhee, William N. 1963. *Formal Theories of Mass Behavior*. New York: Free Press.

McVeigh, Rory, Daniel J. Myers, and David Sikkink. 2004. "Corn, Klansmen, and Coolidge: Structure and Framing in Social Movements." *Social Forces* 83 (2): 653–90.

Mendelberg, Tali. 2001. *The Race Card: Campaign Strategy, Implicit Messages, and the Norm of Equality*. Princeton, NJ: Princeton University Press.

Mendelberg, Tali, Katherine McCabe, and Adam Thal. 2017. "College Socialization and the Economic Views of Affluent Americans." *American Journal of Political Science* 61 (3): 606–23.

Miller, Ronald. 2016. "In Memoriam: Abner J. Mikva (1926–2016)." *University of Chicago Law Review* 83:1739–42.

Minkoff, Debra C. 1997. "The Sequencing of Social Movements." *American Sociological Review* 62 (5): 779–79.

Mondale, Walter, and Morgan Ginther. 2014. "The Mississippi Delegation Debate at the 1964 Democratic National Convention: An Interview with Former Vice President Walter Mondale." *Southern Cultures* 20 (4): 106–15.

Morris, Aldon D. 1984. *The Origins of the Civil Rights Movement: Black Communities Organizing for Change*. New York: Free Press.

Mosley, Ronnie. 2018. "This Is How We Prevent Gun Violence." Email. February 26.

Naim, Moises. 2014. "Why Street Protests Don't Work." *Atlantic*, April 7. Accessed July 19, 2019. https://www.theatlantic.com/international/archive/2014/04/why-street-protests-dont-work/360264/.

Olzak, Susan, and Sarah A. Soule. 2009. "Cross-Cutting Influences of Environmental Protest and Legislation." *Social Forces* 88 (1): 201–25.

Page, Benjamin I., Larry M. Bartels, and Jason Seawright. 2013. "Democracy and the Policy Preferences of Wealthy Americans." *Perspectives on Politics* 11 (1): 51–73.

Page, Benjamin I., and Robert Y. Shapiro. 1992. *The Rational Public: Fifty Years of Trends in Americans' Policy Preferences*. Chicago: University of Chicago Press.

Parker, Christopher S. 2009. *Fighting for Democracy: Black Veterans and the Struggle against White Supremacy in the Postwar South*. Princeton, NJ: Princeton University Press.

Parker, Christopher S., and Matt Barreto. 2013. *Change They Can't Believe In: The Tea Party and Reactionary Politics in America*. Princeton, NJ: Princeton University Press.

Petrocik, John R. 1996. "Issue Ownership in Presidential Elections, with a 1980 Case Study." *American Journal of Political Science* 40 (3): 825–50.

Petrocik, John R., William L. Benoit, and Glenn J. Hansen. 2003–4. "Issue Ownership and Presidential Campaigning, 1952–2000." *Political Science Quarterly* 118 (4): 599–626.

Poole, Keith T., and Thomas Romer. 1985. "Patterns of Political Action Committee Contributions to the 1980 Campaigns for the United States House of Representatives." *Public Choice* 47 (1): 63–111.

Pressman, Jeremy, and Erica Chenoweth. 2019. "About." Crowd Counting Consortium. Accessed January 15, 2019. https://sites.google.com/view/crowdcountingconsortium/about.

Prior, Markus. 2006. "The Incumbent in the Living Room: The Rise of Television and the Incumbency Advantage in U.S. House Elections." *Journal of Politics* 68 (3): 657–73.

Rabinowitz, George, and Stuart Elaine Macdonald. 1989. "A Directional Theory of Issue Voting." *American Political Science Review* 83 (1): 93–121.

Rawls, John. 1971. *A Theory of Justice*. Cambridge, MA: Belknap Press of Harvard University Press.

Rojas, Fabio, and Michael Heaney. 2015. *Party in the Street: The Antiwar Movement and the Democratic Party after 9/11*. New York: Cambridge University Press.

Rosenberg, Nicholas, Ben Bostwick, Tassin Braverman, and Max Senechal. 2017. "The Landscape of Campaign Contributions." Committee for Economic

Development, July 10. Accessed November 11, 2018. https://www.ced.org/reports/single/the-landscape-of-campaign-contributions1.

Rosenstone, Steven J., and John Mark Hansen. 1993. *Mobilization, Participation, and Democracy in America*. New York: Macmillan.

Rustin, Bayard. 1965. "From Protest to Politics: The Future of the Civil Rights Movement." *Commentary* 39 (2).

Sanders, Sam. 2016. "Trump Champions the 'Silent Majority,' But What Does That Mean in 2016?" npr.org. Accessed September 17, 2018. https://www.npr.org/2016/01/22/463884201/trump-champions-the-silent-majority-but-what-does-that-mean-in-2016.

Schattschneider, Elmer E. 1960. *The Semisovereign People: A Realist's View of Democracy in America*. New York: Holt, Rinehart and Winston.

Shingles, Richard D. 1981. "Black Consciousness and Political Participation: The Missing Link." *American Political Science Review* 75 (1): 76–91.

Sigelman, Lee. 1982. "The Nonvoting Voter in Voting Research." *American Political Science Review* 26 (1): 47–56.

Sigelman, Lee, and Emmett H. Buell. 2004. "Avoidance or Engagement? Issue Convergence in U.S. Presidential Campaigns, 1960–2000." *American Journal of Political Science* 48 (4): 650–61.

Smiley, David, and Joey Flechas. 2018. "A Florida Governor's Debate So Intense a Racial Slur Was Spelled Out on Live TV." *Miami Herald*, October 24. Accessed July 19, 2019. https://www.miamiherald.com/news/politics-government/election/article220478140.html.

Snow, David A., E. Burke Rochford, Steven K. Worden, and Robert D. Benford. 1986. "Frame Alignment Processes, Micromobilization, and Movement Participation." *American Sociological Review* 51 (4): 464–81.

Sobieraj, Sarah. 2010. "Reporting Conventions: Journalists, Activists, and the Thorny Struggle for Political Visibility." *Social Problems* 57 (4): 505–28.

———. 2011. *Soundbitten: The Perils of Media-Centered Political Activism*. New York: NYU Press.

Soule, Sarah A. 2009. *Contention and Corporate Social Responsibility*. New York: Cambridge University Press.

———. 2018. "Social Movements and Their Impact on Business and Management." Accessed July 21, 2019. https://oxfordre.com/business/view/10.1093/acrefore/9780190224851.001.0001/acrefore-9780190224851-e-143?print=pdf.

Soule, Sarah A., and Christian Davenport. 2009. "Velvet Glove, Iron Fist, or Even Hand? Protest Policing in the United States, 1960–1990." *Mobilization* 14 (1): 1–22.

Soule, Sarah A., and Jennifer Earl. 2005. "A Movement Society Evaluated: Collective Protest in the United States, 1960–1986." *Mobilization* 10 (3): 345–64.

Soule, Sarah A., Doug McAdam, John McCarthy, and Yang Su. 1999. "Protest Events: Cause or Consequence of State Action. The U.S. Women's Movement and Federal Congressional Activities, 1956–1979." *Mobilization* 4 (2): 239–56.

Sprague, John. 1982. "Is There a Micro Theory Consistent with Contextual Analysis." In *Strategies of Political Inquiry*, edited by Elinor Ostrom, 99–121. Beverly Hills, CA: Sage.

Srnicek, Nick, and Alex Williams. 2015. *Inventing the Future: Postcapitalism and a World without Work*. London: Verso Books.

Stratmann, Thomas. 1991. "What Do Campaign Contributions Buy? Deciphering Causal Effects of Money and Votes." *Southern Economic Journal* 57 (3): 606–20.

———. 2002. "Can Special Interests Buy Congressional Votes? Evidence from Financial Services Legislation." *Journal of Law and Economics* 45 (2): 345–73.

Sulkin, Tracy. 2005. *Issue Politics in Congress*. New York: Cambridge University Press.

Sundquist, James L. 1983. *Dynamics of the Party System: Alignment and Realignment of Political Parties in the United States*. Washington, DC: Brookings Institution.

Tarrow, Sidney G. 1994. *Power in Movement: Social Movements, Collective Action, and Politics*. New York: Cambridge University Press.

———. 1998. *Power in Movement: Social Movements and Contentious Politics*. New York: Cambridge University Press.

———. 2011. *Power in Movement: Social Movements and Contentious Politics*. New York: Cambridge University Press.

Tilly, Charles. 1978. *From Mobilization to Revolution*. Boston: Addison-Wesley.

———. 1996. *Citizenship, Identity and Social History*. Cambridge: Cambridge University Press.

Todorov, Alexander, Anesu N. Mandisodza, Amir Goren, and Crystal C. Hall. 2005. "Inferences of Competence from Faces Predict Election Outcomes." *Science* 308 (5728): 1623–26.

Troy, Tevi. 2016. "The Evolution of Party Conventions." *National Affairs* (Summer). Accessed July 21, 2019. https://www.nationalaffairs.com/publications/detail/the-evolution-of-party-conventions.

Trump, Donald. 2017. "Remarks by President Trump in Roundtable with County Sheriffs." Remarks made in the Roosevelt Room, White House, Washington, DC, February 7.

Truthdig. 2018. "Help Truthdig Cover Activism." Accessed December 3, 2018. https://www.gofundme.com/michael-nigo-poor-people039s-campaign.

Valentino, Nicholas A., and David O. Sears. 2005. "Old Times There Are Not Forgotten: Race and Partisan Realignment in the Contemporary South." *American Journal of Political Science* 49 (3): 672–88.

Van Dyke, Nella. 2003. "Crossing Movement Boundaries: Factors That Facilitate Coalition Protest by American College Students, 1930–1990." *Social Problems* 50 (2): 226–50.

Verba, Sidney, Kay Lehman Schlozman, and Henry E. Brady. 1995. *Voice and Equality: Civic Voluntarism in American Politics*. Cambridge, MA: Harvard University Press.

Weisberg, Herbert F., and Smith Charles E. 1991. "The Influence of the Economy on Party Identification in the Reagan Years." *Journal of Politics* 53 (4): 1077–92.

White, Micah. 2017. "Occupy and Black Lives Matter Failed. We Can Either Win Wars or Win Elections." *Guardian*, August 28. Accessed July 19, 2019. https://www.theguardian.com/commentisfree/2017/aug/29/why-are-our-protests-failing-and-how-can-we-achieve-social-change-today.

Wildavsky, Aaron. 1965. "The Goldwater Phenomenon: Purists, Politicians, and the Two-Party System." *Review of Politics* 27 (3): 386–413.

Wilson, James Q. 1973. *Political Organizations*. Princeton, NJ: Princeton University Press.

Winders, B. 1999. "The Roller Coaster of Class Conflict: Class Segments, Mass Mobilization, and Voter Turnout in the U.S., 1840–1996." *Social Forces* 77 (3): 833–62.

Wright, J Skelly. 1976. "Politics and the Constitution: Is Money Speech?" *Yale Law Journal* 85 (8): 1001–21.

Young, Lisa. 1996. "Women's Movements and Political Parties." *Party Politics* 2 (2): 229–50.

Zald, Mayer N., and D. McCarthy John. 1980. "Social Movement Industries: Competition and Conflict amongst Social Movement Organizations." In *Research in Social Movements, Conflict, and Change*, edited by Louis Kriesberg, 3:1–20. Greenwich, CT: JAI Press.

Zschirnt, Simon. 2011. "The Origins and Meaning of Liberal/Conservative Self-Identifications Revisited." *Political Behavior* 33 (4): 685–701.

INDEX